GETTING I

Housing

FIRST EDITION

DEBBY OUNSTED

TROTMAN

Getting into Housing

This first edition published in 2002
by Trotman and Company Ltd
2 The Green, Richmond, Surrey TW9 1PL

© Trotman and Company Limited and Inside Housing 2002

British Library Cataloguing in Publication Data
A catalogue record for this book is available from the
British Library.

ISBN 0 85660 838 6

Typeset by Mac Style Ltd, Scarborough, N. Yorkshire

CONTENTS

ABOUT THE AUTHOR

Debby Ounsted has worked in housing and local government for 30 years. She tends to keep quiet about her MA in Modern and Medieval Languages, but found her Certificate in Housing Association Finance and her Diploma in Publishing useful in her housing career. She has been Chief Executive of Habinteg Housing Association and of Octavia Hill Housing Trust where she introduced the Investors in People programme that enabled many staff to have better opportunities for personal and career development. Debby has lost track of the number of people she has recruited into housing associations and whose careers she has seen blossom!

She has served on the boards of several housing associations and organisations concerned with disability and for six years chaired the national charity KIDS, which works with children with special needs and their families. She serves currently on the Care Services and the Finance and Personnel Committees of the Joseph Rowntree Foundation and on the Management Committee of the Mercers Housing Association.

Debby now works as a freelance consultant and lives in London with her husband and two children.

ACKNOWLEDGEMENTS

Many people and organisations have contributed to this book. They share a real enthusiasm for housing as a career and a genuine desire to encourage new, young talent into the sector.

Special thanks are due to John Wright and Kate Murray of Inside Housing; Amanda Williams and Rachel Lockhart at Trotman; Martin Winn, Roger Keller, Melanie Rees, Jill Goult and Heather Finch and all their colleagues at the Chartered Institute of Housing; to Peter Jeffery at Genesis Housing Group; to Adrian Moran and colleagues at the Housing Corporation; to Jane Greenoak and Barbara Regnier at the National Housing Federation; to Joseph Ogbonna at Family Housing Association; to Gerry Dryden at Heart of England Housing Group; to Chris Root and Karen Bennison at Places for People; Sally Jacobson and Dyane Kesto at London and Quadrant Housing Group, to Nigel Sprigings at Salford University, to David Hewitt at ARMA and to many others for sharing their stories about why they came to work in housing. And especially to Jenny Walsh for her skill and patience in turning the raw material into readable form.

Sponsors

We are very grateful to our sponsors, Capita, Genesis Housing Group, Home Group, and the Housing Corporation.

The views in this book are those of the author and do not necessarily reflect those of other organisations.

Housing Corporation IGP Database Ref No G0105638

GLOSSARY

Affidavit	A legal document signed under oath made as part of Court proceedings
Arrears	Rent or other charges owed to a landlord
Eviction/Possession proceedings	The legal process of taking back a property from a tenant who has failed to abide by their side of the tenancy agreement (usually because of failure to pay the rent), or of removing someone who has occupied a property illegally, such as a squatter
Fixtures and fittings	Items which are fixed to the property (such as light sockets and radiators) which the landlord is responsible for, as opposed to furniture or other items which usually belong to and are the responsibility of the tenant
Housing benefit	Government-funded financial support towards the cost of housing, payable to people with low or no income
Housing Corporation	The body sponsored by the government's Department for Transport, Local Government and the Regions to register, regulate and fund the work of housing associations
Key workers	Public sector employees such as teachers and nurses whose incomes may be too low for them to afford to purchase property in reasonable distance of their work-place
Lettings policy	A description of how people will be selected for particular properties, which usually takes into account the extent of their current housing difficulties
Loss adjusters	Those who assess how much should be paid out by an insurance company on a claim, particularly when the amount claimed is disputed

LSVT associations	large scale voluntary transfer associations. These are newly formed housing associations set up to take over the management of properties previously owned by councils
National Housing Federation	The trade body for housing associations that promotes their work and represents their views to government
Nuisance	This is hard to be precise about, but is the term used for annoyance or hurt caused (for which there is sometimes legal remedy) when one resident or group of residents is disturbed on a regular basis by another, for example by loud music being played late at night
Service charges	Amounts charged to tenants, in addition to the rent, which pay for particular services such as gardening of communal landscaping, electricity used for lighting common halls and stairways, maintenance of lifts in blocks of flats
Specification	The detailed technical description which sets out for a building contractor what work is to be done
Tenancy agreement	The contract signed between landlord and tenant setting out their mutual responsibilities and rights
Tendering	The process of asking several contractors to offer a price for a piece of building work, with a view to making sure that value for money is being obtained
Tenure	The legal term for the method by or conditions on which you occupy your home
Void property	An empty property

SPONSOR'S INTRODUCTION

There are few industries which offer career opportunities as diverse as housing. Greater challenges face people who work in the sector now than ever before. Heavy demand, higher expectations from customers and the need to keep a firm hand on costs makes running the social enterprise called 'Housing' a complex and demanding job.

Housing organisations build strong relationships with their customers. They provide excellent services to people who live in their properties and constantly seek to improve what they do. At the same time their businesses are growing and they have to keep their costs down. The social housing industry is thriving but it needs people with creativity, flair and drive to meet the enormous challenges of the 21st century.

There are many professions involved in the task and many skills can be transferred between the public and the private housing sectors. So housing can offer great job mobility as your career develops.

The Capita Group plc, a FTSE 100 company and leading professional support services organisation, offers a range of specialist corporate services designed to help meet the demands facing the housing industry. The wide range of services offered include construction, consultancy, IT services, accounting and recruitment.

Capita Social Housing Resourcing is part of the Capita Group and has over 14 years experience finding skilled housing professionals. As a market leader in professional recruitment and training it handles full- and part-time, temporary, fixed term and permanent recruitment positions, from administrators and surveyors through to senior management executives.

This stimulating handbook provides you with a taster of what a career in housing could mean for you. I wish you every success with your search.

Dennis Markey
Director, Capita Social Housing Resourcing

Home
GROUP

OPPORTUNITIES WITH HOME GROUP

The **Home Group** is one of the UK's leading providers of rented housing, supported housing and low cost home ownership through its subsidiaries throughout the country.

We employ almost 2,200 people to manage our 45,000 properties and develop our programme of 1,800 new homes every year.

Whether you're interested in Architecture or Accountancy; Housing or Human Resources; Property Surveying or Public Relations there are opportunities for you within our organisation.

Home Housing Association provides development, management and maintenance services to almost 23,000 homes throughout the North of England, Yorkshire and the Midlands.

Warden Housing Association works in over 90 local authority areas across the South of England managing over 11,500 homes.

Stonham Housing Association is Britain's largest provider of housing, care and support services for people with special needs. Stonham offers support to over 6,000 people each year.

Paramount Homes provides market rent properties and associated commercial services in stock owned by equity investors as well as Home Group.

Home in Scotland manages and develops homes north of the Border.

Home Group has an active Training and Development programme and has Investors in People accreditation.

For further information on how to get a job in housing, write to: Human Resources Department, Home Group Ltd, Ridley House, Regent Centre, Gosforth, Newcastle upon Tyne NE3 3JE.

FOREWORD

Everyone needs a decent home in which to live. Building and managing rented housing is a complex profession and there is an enormous variety on the kinds of jobs available. From advising people who need a place to live and those who collect the rent and arrange repairs, to those who care for older and vulnerable residents – these and many more help people provide a home for themselves and their families. There can be few other jobs where your daily work can transform other people's lives so directly.

Now is an exciting time to start a career in housing as it is not restricted to managing rented accommodation alone. Revitalising the older parts of cities and helping rural communities to flourish represent some of the major challenges which housing professionals now face and where you could really make a difference.

Getting into Housing gives you a taster of the diversity of what housing organisations do. Opportunities for interesting and really enjoyable work abound, and training and personal development goes with it.

Leaving school? Not sure what to do? Looking for a change of direction or wanting to do something worthwhile? You really can make an impact by choosing a career in housing.

David Butler
Chief Executive
Chartered Institute of Housing

Kate Murray
Editor
Inside Housing

Innovative
Stimulating
Diverse
Challenging
Rewarding

That's the reality of a career in one of the many Housing Association Groups across the UK.

In a recent survey, over 70% of people said working for a Housing Association would make a real difference to people's lives. They were right, and Genesis Housing Group is no exception. As a leading housing charity there are over 100,000 people across London who have a home… when they might otherwise be on the streets.

From neighbourhood housing officers to architects and from community development officers to customer service reps, there's a job you'll love right here, right now. And if all that's not enough, we also offer a competitive salary, pension scheme and brilliant job security.

Most of all though, we offer the chance to change people's lives for good.

For more information about a career at Genesis Housing Group, call the Director of HR on 020 8537 412 or e-mail us at jobs@ghg.org.uk, **quoting ref: GIH1**.

Genesis Housing Group Ltd
Registered Office: Canterbury House, Canterbury Road, London NW6 5SQ
Housing Corporation No. L4286
Company Number: 3802456

GENESIS
HOUSING GROUP

INTRODUCTION – REVITALISING NEIGHBOURHOODS

'Somewhere to live'

We all need somewhere to live. The quality of where we live has a real impact on our lives and on our children's prospects. While most people in Britain own their own homes, 7.5 million people live in rented accommodation. This may be because they prefer renting or because they cannot afford to buy.

Revitalising neighbourhoods

Bringing life back into run-down neighbourhoods is a real challenge, as much in the inner cities as in rural communities. Most people in Britain enjoy a much higher standard of living and greater prosperity than ever before. But millions of children and adults are still excluded from this general trend. There are some pockets of real deprivation where poor housing and education, lack of jobs and high crime rates lead to serious social stress and a cycle of disadvantage for the people who live there. Housing organisations are now at the heart of the partnerships with residents, helping change the face of poorer Britain and putting real opportunity for a better quality of life within reach of all.

Creativity, flair and drive

The government is determined to transform public services and it needs people with creativity, flair and drive to meet this challenge.

The range of jobs available and the skills and qualities needed to play a part in this transformation is enormous. This book is about the sort of work involved in helping people get suitable housing and improving the quality of life for people living in less well-off areas, about the kinds of people you might work with and the career paths you might follow.

1

WHAT DO WE MEAN BY 'HOUSING'?

Local councils and housing associations own 5.3 million properties that they let, often at a rent well below the private sector rent level, to people who are on their lists or are homeless. Building homes, letting to tenants, collecting the rent, doing the repairs, solving neighbourhood problems, helping families who need to move and keeping estates clean and tidy is a surprisingly big and complicated undertaking.

Many estates and housing schemes built by local authorities and housing associations are lovely places to live, with good local services and are popular with new applicants. But parts of some towns and cities have very poor housing. The quality of life and the prospects for people who live there can be dismal. A mixture of things can make a neighbourhood go downhill: lack of work, below average schools, bad public transport, lack of places for recreation, poor security and so on. In some parts of the country the 'housing market' has collapsed both in the privately owned and the rented sectors; estates have become hard to find tenants for because the environment has become so poor and many tenants need extra help and support if they are specially disadvantaged or have health problems. People who can afford to get out may vote with their feet. It can be a real downward spiral for those who are left behind.

Helping to tackle these major problems creates some of the most challenging jobs around today. Where major city regeneration projects are under way tenants often have to move so that extensive modernisation can be carried out, redundant buildings demolished and new community facilities, shops and offices provided. This means arranging temporary moves and this brings the danger of breaking up well-established community networks, with all the disruption which that entails. Good liaison between all the different bodies concerned is essential – regional government and local councils, businesses and banks, schools, health and education workers, social services and the police all have a part to play. And obtaining grants and loans from all sorts of different government and private financiers to do the work is a job in itself.

Meanwhile there are many neighbourhoods where 'prevention' is what matters most – making sure that there is enough intelligent investment in the community to ensure it doesn't collapse if the local economy is put under pressure, for example if a big local employer moves out.

This whole enterprise is often given the shorthand title 'social housing' or the more up-beat name 'affordable housing'. Around 115,000 people are employed by housing associations in England in providing and managing such housing, and this is set to double in the next five years. When you add in people employed by councils, in housing benefit administration, the private sector, institutional landlords and so on, the figure is said to be around 650,000 people. So you can see that job opportunities abound.

And 25,000 new homes to rent are being built with the help of public grants every year. There are also lots of private landlords, some just starting to let their property without any government subsidy. Decent housing for everyone is at the heart of public social policy, because it is recognised that good housing plays a fundamental part in individual health and well-being, together with the more talked about subjects of education and health. But because housing does not catch much media attention it has often been overlooked as a career by people who want to have a social purpose in their work.

An exciting time to get involved

It is an exciting time to get involved in housing with all the changes and improvements that are happening. The government is backing councils and housing associations to make a real impact on run-down neighbourhoods. Over the next few years this 'regeneration' work will have a high profile and there will be resources to help make dramatic improvements, working with the people who live there to make their future prospects brighter.

Green issues and sustainable housing

There is also a real interest in 'green' issues that relate to housing. Making sure that new homes are energy efficient and use materials wisely is only part of the task. Making sure people can afford to heat and light their homes is part of it too.

Everyone has an interest in improving the environment and this includes areas where there are many council and housing association homes.

'I WORK IN HOUSING'

When people say 'I work in housing,' they may be doing anything from helping a homeless family into their first permanent home, collecting rent, or organising a huge renovation programme in a tower block.

Many black and ethnic minority families live in disproportionately poor housing compared to the rest of the population. There are a number of housing associations led by people from ethnic minorities who recognise the special challenges of getting real equality of opportunity for people who may be disadvantaged because of their ethnic origin. If you work for an organisation with housing in a multiracial area you may be working to develop better links and relationships between community groups.

You might have a job in a rural community, helping to provide homes that local people, perhaps on a low agricultural wage, can afford. Housing and economic stress can be just as acute in the country, especially when transport links are poor and buying a home is pricey. Whether you want to work in one of the big conurbations, or whether you prefer the country, you will find there are great opportunities for getting into housing as a career. What is shared by everyone involved in housing is the common purpose of helping people to get a decent place to live and helping them to enjoy their home as long as they stay.

Are you about to leave school?

This wide variety in the kinds of jobs available means a wide range of qualities, skills, competencies and qualifications needed to do them. Many of the skills that school leavers or students may have developed doing holiday jobs, for example the ability to communicate well with people at all levels, the ability to do tasks on time and to see tasks through to the end, will be a good grounding for work in housing.

Thinking of a career change?

You may be reading this book because you are thinking about a career move in later life, or going back to work after a career break. One of the best things about housing is that it welcomes incomers from different backgrounds. You are less likely to be discriminated against because of your age when looking for a new job. This is because housing organisations are generally scrupulous in applying best recruitment practice when looking for new staff. They want the best person for the job, and they recognise the importance of life experience in a career that is essentially about people.

You might be an accountant in the City, or in marketing, or a surveyor, and you might feel that there must be more to life than working for just the profit motive. In Chapter 9 there are plenty of examples of interesting and worthwhile jobs in other professions that play an essential part in the success of housing organisations. Being able to transfer your experience and skills into this enjoyable sector is well worth considering.

CAREER PROSPECTS

Prospects for a satisfying career in housing have never been better. Housing Potential UK is the government's skills agency for the housing sector. In the spring of 2002 it launched a workforce development plan, commissioned by the Department for Education and Skills, which sets out what action is needed to recruit, retain and develop a suitably buoyant workforce for housing in the 21st century, not just for subsidised rented housing but for private renting and managing different kinds of rented housing as well. Their website at www.housingpotential.com is well worth visiting to find out more.

Training and career development

Councils and housing associations are generally keen to help all staff develop their careers and there is often support available for a variety of courses, from HNC through to postgraduate and Chartered Institute of Housing professional qualifications. Many employers have the Investors in People badge, which means they really are committed to giving employees the best possible chance to get a lot out of their work. Of all staff, 9.7 per cent come from black and minority ethnic backgrounds and housing organisations are committed to offering equal opportunities to all.

In-house training and external courses are usually provided for staff. There is a lot of job mobility between employers. Someone might start work as a trainee with a housing association, move on to a council's housing department and move on later to a government body or another association on promotion. Some employers have only a handful of staff, others have a cast of thousands. So there are great opportunities for working in different parts of the country and getting a variety of experience.

CASE STUDY

Jenny Allinson of Home Housing Association, acting housing manager

Jenny Allinson couldn't have foreseen her career with the Home Group when she first encountered the organisation in the mid-nineties. Whilst studying at the University of Northumbria Jenny was 'recruited' to act as a 'guinea pig' interviewee for training purposes and little did she know that seven years later she would be appointed as Acting Housing Manager covering a patch of almost 4000 houses.

Following the completion of her degree in social sciences she decided to take a postgraduate diploma in housing policy: she became interested in housing during a module on homelessness in her final year. Jenny joined Home for her second year placement in June 95.

Jenny had been impressed with her time at Home, particularly the continuous training she received as well as the practical hands-on work dealing with all aspects of housing management within the company, so she kept her eye out in the local press for any vacancies and in June 1996 successfully applied for a job as a tenants services officer at one of Home's local offices in Newcastle upon Tyne.

Jenny's enthusiasm for housing was encouraged by her colleagues and in August 1998, with two years experience under her belt, she was promoted to the role of assistant housing manager which allowed her to continue to deal face to face with tenants but also gave her the chance to become more involved in decision making at a local level.

In March this year she was appointed acting housing manager for the whole of the Wearside region.

Her success has been encouraged by Home. The group has a thriving training and development programme for all its staff and Jenny has recently completed a seven month management development programme; she is currently training to be a qualified facilitator; and was instrumental in successfully co-ordinating our bid for Investors in People accreditation.

Jenny has also recently married one of her colleagues so she counts her time with Home Group an unqualified success!

YOU can make a real difference

Housing appeals as a career because young people can make a real practical impact from the very start. As soon as they try to leave home, school leavers and students understand at first hand how hard it is to find a place to live and what a difference good housing makes. Housing employers often look for potential, rather than long track records, and are genuinely committed to being equal opportunity employers, seeking to get the best from their workforce. Staff in housing teams are enthusiastic and energetic, enjoying the challenge of a practical job with a serious social purpose.

HOW THIS BOOK IS ARRANGED

Because all councils and associations have different numbers of properties to look after, the way in which the work is arranged will vary from place to place. The names given to jobs also differ from employer to employer. For example, a customer services adviser in one place might be doing much the same as a repairs assistant in another. Policies and priorities also vary tremendously, so this book should be taken as a general guide. But each job will have a written explanation of what the work and the responsibilities entail. This is usually called a job description. It's important to look at what it says in the job description, rather than just the title of the job, when deciding whether or not a particular post is for you.

Each chapter in this book describes the different sorts of functions there are to be performed. If you work in Scotland, Wales or Northern Ireland the terminology, funding and administrative structures will be slightly different. Devolution to all parts of the UK will mean that changes will continue to be introduced. The appropriate office of the Chartered Institute of Housing, or the national equivalents of the Housing Corporation in England (addresses are given at the back of this book), can give you more information. But you will find the jobs described broadly available from landlords – both public and private – throughout the UK.

A word on **jargon**. As in most professions, people in housing love talking in jargon, using shorthand for complicated terms and initials for long-winded names. We don't realise we're doing it most of the time! Although this book has tried to simplify and explain things, there is also a glossary on pages vi and vii that should help.

CASE STUDY

Sally Jacobson is the Personnel and Training Director at London and Quadrant Housing Group. Sally moved into housing from the NHS 15 years ago. She says 'What could be more fundamental to health than good housing, and where else could you make such a difference every day of your working life? When you work in housing you know that you are playing a part in transforming lives. That is true whether you work on the front line, or in finance or in personnel and training like myself. We are all part of the team. It's fantastically busy and we encourage anyone who wants a satisfying career and to make a real contribution to give it a try.'

BACKGROUND – AN INDUSTRY OVERVIEW

Before thinking about what's involved in working in housing, you need to have an idea about what different kinds of organisations provide it, how they are run and who they are accountable to for the quality of what they do. The thing to remember is that there are huge changes afoot, with residents as 'customers' becoming ever more involved and influential in deciding how things should be done.

WHAT IS COUNCIL HOUSING?

Local authorities or councils are run by elected councillors who normally represent a political party. The party with the most councillors decides what is to be spent on which activities each year. Councils employ paid staff and may be one of the biggest employers in their area. They are responsible for a wide variety of services. These can include:

- education
- libraries and leisure
- social services
- refuse collection and street cleaning
- environmental matters such as air and noise pollution
- planning
- licensing shops, pubs and restaurants

and, of course, housing. They have an important role in forming the strategies for what is to be done in their area, through local strategic partnerships.

They collect a council tax from every household and rates from each business in their area and this, together with income from people who use their services and money from the government goes to cover the cost of what they do. They administer housing benefit, which helps people with no or low incomes to pay for their housing. Councils also provide and manage permanent houses and flats to rent, and must give help to people who are homeless. Council housing has to meet standards approved by the Audit Commission's housing inspectorate who, like school inspectors, examine the quality of what is done each year and suggest areas for improvement.

Some councils run their housing directly themselves. Some have passed their properties over to be run by housing associations after a tenants' vote (see 'LSVTs' in the next section). In some organisations tenants are in charge of ensuring that the standards of housing management are up to scratch through tenant management organisations.

WHAT IS A HOUSING ASSOCIATION?

Housing associations are independent voluntary organisations that, unlike private companies, do not exist to make a profit for shareholders. Their main purpose is to provide housing for people in need. Many associations are registered as charities. They are governed by a board or committee of management whose members are not paid for the work they do. They are volunteers. They are likely to have expertise from their own working lives that they bring to help guide the work of their association. More and more associations have tenants on their boards who have direct experience of the quality of their landlord's work.

The board oversees the policy and direction of the association's work and usually employs paid professional staff to carry it out. The money they need to build houses and do their other work comes partly from the rents they collect, partly from the government via a body called the Housing Corporation, in England, and partly from private loans. There are more than 2000 associations which are registered with the Housing Corporation. This means their standards of work have been checked and they are thought fit to receive government support.

There are about 500 larger, active associations that are building new homes and are involved in regeneration work. Some of them are huge, with more than 50,000 homes; they work all over the country, employing thousands of staff. Some have just a handful of homes and one or two employees.

Some are based in just one or two boroughs and might be involved in other activities as well as housing, such as community work and employment and training initiatives. Some specialise in helping particular groups of vulnerable people, for example frail elderly people, or young adults with learning disabilities. Many work in towns where the population includes people from black and minority ethnic groups. Many associations are very small, and might for example run just one long-established almshouse or a hostel in a rural village.

Many councils are transferring their properties across to be managed by new housing associations set up specifically for that purpose. These are known as LSVT associations (large scale voluntary transfer associations). They concentrate on working with tenants in the district to upgrade the former council housing stock and look for new local housing and regeneration possibilities.

DIFFERENT KINDS OF HOUSING ORGANISATIONS

You may have heard of other names for organisations involved in housing – cooperatives, housing action trusts, tenant management organisations, housing companies and arm's length management organisations, for example.

There are also plenty of housing jobs within the private sector, working as a managing agent for small landlords or institutions that own property which is let or leased privately and not built with the help of public money. The legislation is different but the skills are relevant. Another obviously related career is within estate agency, selling homes to people who prefer to purchase rather than rent their homes.

Within the council and housing association sector there is a great deal of scope for learning about different forms of home ownership. Council tenants and others have had the 'right to buy' the property they live in for some years, which means that there may be a mixture of tenures within one group of properties. 'Tenure' is the word used to describe the method through which you occupy your home, whether as a tenant, freeholder or leaseholder. In blocks of flats some people may have weekly tenancies and others may have purchased a long lease for say 99 years (with the right to sell on). Managing blocks where residents have different tenures is especially demanding and is a good training ground if you want to work in the private sector later.

Many housing associations offer different forms of home ownership aimed at people with relatively low incomes but who want to get a stake in the value of their home, for example shared ownership and leasehold schemes for elderly people.

It is not within the scope of this book to go into the detail of how all these different organisations arrange their work. But the types of jobs described will pop up in different guises and with different names in most housing organisations. All offer examples of the real potential for exciting and challenging work in housing today, and learning your way round in one organisation will equip you well for developing your career further in another, as so many of the skills you will learn are transferable.

PART ONE: CAREER CHOICES

CASE STUDY

Kamaran Mirza, Neighbourhood Housing Officer, Genesis Housing Group

'Genesis gave me the opportunity and I proved myself ... every day I go home and I know that I've done something good.'

Kamaran tells his story:

After finishing my degree in 1998, I started working as a graphic designer almost straight away. The money was brilliant, but it soon became clear that I wasn't cut out for a job where I was based in the office for 8 hours every day, so I decided to take the opportunity to do something a little different.

That's when I first thought about working for a housing association, helping to provide homes for thousands of people who might not otherwise have one.

I joined PCHA (part of the Genesis Housing Group) in April 1999, as an administration officer. It wasn't quite what I wanted to do because it was still totally office based, but I did know that at Genesis there might be a chance to work in other areas.

I'm a people person, so it was always going to be important to me to have lots of regular contact with a wide range of people. That's the beauty of working for Genesis, where there are loads of career paths covering every possible angle you can think of. So, when I had the chance to join the trainee housing officer programme, I jumped at it.

Genesis gave me the opportunity and I proved myself! Now, just under two years later, I'm a fully qualified neighbourhood housing officer, and I love it! My role is to be the first point of contact for many of the Genesis Housing Group's thousands of tenants. I deal with everything from housing issues to just being a good listener. And there's loads of opportunity to get involved with community development stuff, working with kids and a really broad-based, diverse community.

It's pretty challenging stuff and every day throws something new at me, but the training programme at Genesis is excellent and my colleagues are all really, really supportive. I'm always trying to improve myself and give the best service I can and it helps that I get on brilliantly with the tenants.

Basically, every day I go home thinking that I've done something good.

Chapter 1
WORKING IN NEIGHBOURHOOD MANAGEMENT

Both councils and housing associations employ staff in a variety of positions to carry out the complicated job of managing property. The emphasis nowadays is on the quality of the service given to the residents.

So the phrase used to describe this work, housing management, has often been replaced by 'tenant services', or the much wider term 'neighbourhood management', indicating that people and communities are at the heart of things, rather than just the bricks and mortar.

Here are some of the functions that are commonly undertaken by the tenant services or neighbourhood management department. The term 'assistant' (for example lettings assistant) is frequently used for someone doing fairly routine administrative duties. 'officers' (for example housing officer) may be responsible for a wider range of duties and more involved in decision-making. Teams of officers will usually be headed up by a manager who is likely to be professionally qualified, and in turn managers will report to the director of the whole department.

LETTINGS OR ALLOCATIONS

The responsibilities include:

- Keeping the list of people waiting for homes up to date.
- Keeping a register of which tenants would like or need to transfer to a different property, or to move to a property owned by a different landlord altogether, or to swap their home with a tenant of another landlord (called a 'Mutual Exchange')
- When properties become empty, deciding with colleagues in line with the agreed policy which applicant should be offered the vacancy, taking into account the number of bedrooms and the location and

comparing that with what the applicant both needs and would like.
There are also schemes now to give more choice to applicants.

- Planning who is going to move in to newly built properties that are
  being occupied for the first time.
- Liaising with the local council, which will keep a list of people seeking
  housing in the district and who may have priority for having their
  names put forward to local housing associations. (Most associations
  sign a nominations agreement with their local council to offer a
  proportion of their homes to people on the council list; this is in
  exchange for getting public grants.)
- Liaising with other housing organisations, especially where your
  tenants want to move to a different part of the country or need a size
  of property that your organisation does not have available.
- Keeping required records of who has been housed and where.
- Monitoring how long it takes to relet empty property – keeping the
  length of time a property has been empty ('void') as short as possible is
  a high priority for landlords.
- Feeding back to the design team what tenants like about their homes,
  and what sort of property there is high demand for.
- Liaising with other agencies such as social services if the person being
  housed needs support. This could include attending a case conference
  where a number of agencies come together to coordinate how they can
  work together to help an applicant.

While it can be very satisfying finding a property that really matches
what the applicant wants, working in Lettings can be very stressful
where there is high demand for social housing, because you are often
seen as a gatekeeper, whose main job is to say 'No'.

By contrast in some parts of the country, such as the Midlands and the
North, some areas have become so undesirable that it is hard to let
vacancies at all. Or it may be that the design and facilities in the property
have become outmoded, for example bed-sits with shared bathrooms.
Private flats nearby may have lower rents. Lettings staff have to keep an
eye out for signs that this is beginning to happen. Of course there is the
immediate problem that an empty flat does not generate any rental
income for the landlord. But a bigger concern is all the other problems
that empty flats can bring, such as dereliction, vandalism, squatting and
so on. Lettings staff often need to be imaginative with finding new ways

of making homes appeal, and there are many experiments going on to make the whole process more attractive and effective, giving much greater choice to tenants. Staff will also help the landlord identify which properties need modernisation and updating if they are to continue being acceptable to new generations of tenants.

Skills and qualities

- good communication
- excellent administrative skills with an eye for detail
- fair-mindedness
- sensitivity inside a tough skin!

HOUSING MANAGEMENT – OR TENANT SERVICES

This team's work is at the centre of what every housing organisation does. Staff in housing or estate management are responsible for:

- 'Signing up', which means going through the tenancy agreement with new tenants, making sure they understand what the responsibilities in it imply, sorting out keys, gas and electricity. Usually a detailed tenants' handbook is given out too.
- Helping them move in if needed.
- Arranging furniture if needed.
- Helping people who are applying for housing benefit complete the forms and checking that they understand what their benefit entitlement is.
- Checking that people have settled in and that they know how to handle the basic fixtures in the property, such as the central heating.
- Making sure they know how to report repairs and also which repairs they are expected to do themselves.
- Making sure that rent is paid regularly and on time.
- Making arrangements to collect arrears, including giving benefits advice to help maximise people's incomes.
- Liaising with social services or voluntary support agencies if an individual needs any special kind of support day to day, for example because of mental ill health or because they are increasingly vulnerable through old age.

- Usually managing the caretakers based on the estates, and making sure they have all the supplies they need to keep the surroundings and the communal parts of buildings clean and tidy.
- Responding to complaints from tenants if neighbours cause nuisance or disturbance; this could range from the noise from toddlers' feet in the upstairs flat through late-night rowdy parties to drug dealing or other criminal activity.
- Working through the legal system if a tenant has to be evicted; this is only likely to arise if there are serious and persistent arrears, serious nuisance, or harassment or other criminal behaviour.
- Getting feedback from tenants about the services provided and involving tenants in how their homes are managed.
- Working closely with the development teams when new homes are being designed.

Skills and qualities

You need to be well organised and also a good organiser of others; scrupulously fair-minded, tactful and discreet; firm; robust enough to cope with stressful situations, for which you often can find no answer.

A day in the life of a Housing Officer

8am   In early to get rent chasing letters out to Ms B and Mr Z and check yesterday's rent printout. Ouch, my arrears are up this week.

9am   Bike over to visit Mrs A, new tenant who doesn't speak English. She needs help with understanding how to fill out her benefit claim. Her grandson acts as interpreter. Turns out she's also worried that stairwells are dark. Remind caretaker to adjust timing on the central lights.

10am   Back at office; I'm on a 'Best Value' review group. We are looking at ways of improving how we do things in consultation with our 'customers', the tenants. We're thinking about our service charges. That's the money we have to charge to tenants on top of their rents for things such as communal heating and lighting, caretaking and lifts. If we can streamline the administration and give more accurate details to tenants there'll be fewer complaints and

---

it'll be easier to collect the income we need to cover the costs. It makes sense really.

12 noon   Sandwich man arrives. I'll get a cheese and tomato and a Mars Bar to keep me going; I'm in court this afternoon on an eviction. Bump into the repairs administrator in reception. Remind him Mrs H needs her heating fixed urgently; she's coming out of hospital this afternoon.

Ring the social worker about Mr S. The neighbours say he isn't looking after himself and there's a funny smell coming from his flat. Arrange a visit with the environmental health officer to see if there's a serious problem.

2pm   Go to Court. Luckily I remembered to change into my suit. See some of my friends who are also doing my housing course. Coursework has helped me to understand the legal side of housing better. We didn't think we needed a solicitor on this one as it was straightforward. Judge seems quite sympathetic given the high level of arrears, but I think the fact I did the affidavit so thoroughly helps. Tenant doesn't show up. I think he's done a bunk. We are granted possession. Wonder what'll happen to him. Do diary note to get the flat cleared and secured.

4.30pm   Pop in to see Mrs H on my way back to the office; fantastic; the heating engineers are just leaving; her daughter's there waiting for the ambulance to bring her back. I promise to check everything's OK with the home care team tomorrow.

Back at the office lettings team are pleased about the court result, because the man who's gone was taking up a three-bed house with a garden: they're pure gold dust to the lettings people.

5.30pm   Tenants' association meeting on one of my estates tonight. Should be OK now that noisy tenant has moved away.

Ooh look, I didn't have time to eat the Mars Bar. Funny thing, I once thought of applying to work for them when I was a student. Lots of my friends did. Glad I didn't; housing's more exciting than chocolate. A good day really; several satisfied customers; computer didn't break down; and I'm off on day release tomorrow so I can sleep in.

CASE STUDY

Susie started as a temp on reception at a medium-sized housing association in West London, covering the job for a woman who was on maternity leave. She'd previously worked as a cashier in a bank. She found her training in customer care from the bank really useful in her new position.

She was then asked to cover the post of a housing assistant who was on extended sick leave and made such a success of it that she applied for and got the job permanently when the post-holder decided not to come back to work. She then studied for a BTec, being allowed day release, and meanwhile was promoted to housing officer. She failed one of her papers first time, but persisted and successfully completed the course while she was on six months maternity leave herself. Although she lived more than an hour away from the office she decided to continue commuting to her job when she came back from maternity leave, but kept an eye open for other possibilities closer to home. This was a hard time for her, juggling the day-to-day housing officer visits to sites across London with the need to meet her child care commitments.

The association that employed her then merged with another association and Susie was promoted to a senior position, which was more managerial and office based. She was given the chance to train in the staff managerial skills she needed to develop and has much more flexibility over her day-to-day working arrangements, so as well as gaining a promotion she has also made life a bit easier on the childcare front.

Chapter 2
THE FRONT LINE: CUSTOMER SERVICES

RECEPTION WORK

First impressions of any kind of organisation are important. How customers are treated on the phone and when they visit the office affects significantly what they think of the organisation. Courtesy, thoughtfulness and efficiency from the receptionist who sits at the front desk create a positive image. Housing organisations usually vie with the best to provide a welcoming, fresh and professional front desk service.

'Customers' in the social housing world are a mixture of people. They may be families desperate for a place to live. They may already be tenants who need urgent repairs to their home. They may be elderly people feeling threatened by noisy youths or locals who hold the landlord responsible for everything that goes on in the neighbourhood. They may be other professionals such as social workers, or applicants coming for a job interview.

All housing organisations, councils and associations alike, have daily communication with other official bodies, such as government departments, and Members of Parliament and councillors. Many other people will be in regular phone and personal contact – maintenance contractors, IT installers, delivery people, solicitors, architects, surveyors – the list is endless.

All of these people will be affected by the way they are treated by the person in the council or association they first have contact with. If the receptionist is abrupt or fails to pass on a message, if the person answering the phone is rude or patronising, then the customer will go away with the opinion that everyone who works for that office is like that. Equally, a good experience will create a satisfied customer. Research shows that we are far more likely to tell other people about a bad experience we have had than a good one! So it's vital to get the customer approach as positive, welcoming and efficient as it can be.

Even though much communication now is by email or direct phone line rather than through a switchboard, the bulk of first contact is still through the front line staff. The position really matters.

Arrangements differ, depending on the size of the organisation. A smaller place might have only one or two staff dealing with phone enquiries, handling all reception duties and sometimes doing word processing and central administration as well. Administration could include:

- answering calls and managing the switchboard;
- taking responsibility for opening and distributing the post
- getting the evening post out;
- ensuring that there are up-to-date supplies of rent books and other documentation needed by tenants;
- arranging courier deliveries of important documents;
- keeping track of keys to homes available to be let or where building work is being done;
- taking details of repairs that need to be done;
- keeping track of the office diary, knowing who is where when;
- welcoming guests, keeping the visitors log, escorting people to meetings.

In larger housing organisations there may be much bigger teams using sophisticated IT, acting as customer services officers who are trained to deal on the phone with a wide range of enquiries and problems. Technology may have been installed which makes it easy to identify where a caller lives, what outstanding or previous problems they may have asked you to deal with, what make of equipment is installed in the home, so that it is easier to order spare parts when repairs are needed – there's a lengthy list of useful information computer systems can hold to make the service more efficient.

REPAIRS ORDERING AND ADMINISTRATION

One of the main differences between being a tenant and owning your own place is that a tenant is not usually responsible for repairs to the property: that is the landlord's job.

Once the tenancy agreement has been signed and the new family has moved in repairs are sometimes their only reason to contact the landlord. More than any other aspect of the services offered, the quality of the maintenance affects everyone's opinion of the landlord. And more than anything else poor maintenance sours public opinion, no matter what the reason for it.

Councils and housing associations need to keep their properties in good repair. Not only are they legally obliged to do so, but they want to make sure tenants have a property that is in decent condition. If major faults – such as leaks from water tanks or slipped slates on the roof – are left to fester eventually the damage will be significant. So landlords want to offer a quick and efficient repairs service.

Social landlords publish the standards expected of the speed with which they will do the work: usually emergency repairs – such as a broken front door – might be done on the same day, urgent repairs such as lack of hot water done within 3 days and routine repairs, such as broken fencing or a loose window sash, within 28 days.

The administrators or customer services advisers will usually be responsible for:

- placing an order for routine repairs to be done by an approved contractor or an in-house operator;
- making arrangements for a builder to get in;
- following up the progress on the work (the contractor may have to wait for spare parts, and the tenant will want to be reassured that the job has not been forgotten);
- signing off the job when it is completed so that the invoice can be processed;
- recording and monitoring statistics;
- checking that the tenant is satisfied with the work done.

Skills and qualities

As well as having a genuine desire to help people sort out problems you need to be a good listener – able to probe to get accurate information. You must enjoy the real practicalities of learning how a house and its fixtures and fittings are put together. And you need to be a terrier, determined to see the detail right through to the end. A good telephone manner and a bit of personal charm may smooth the job along too.

Chapter 3
MAINTENANCE AND SURVEYING

The basics of 'housing' are all about bricks and mortar. The biggest asset of any landlord is likely to be the properties he or she owns, aside from the staff, that is! Quite apart from the need to keep the home warm and dry for the benefit of the people who live there a landlord needs to keep property in good repair in order to maintain its value. A house with a leaking roof, rattling window frames and rising damp is going to be less valuable than one in decent condition. This is just as true for a small private landlord as for a council with thousands of homes.

The previous chapter explained the job of the administrators who take calls from residents asking for repairs to be done. Working closely with the administrators are the technical people, the surveyors whose job it is to diagnose the causes of major problems, decide on the cure and make sure the building contractors do the work well.

Some larger housing organisations, especially councils, employ their own in-house labour force of tradesmen with the different skills needed to keep their properties in good repair, and there may be training leading to nationally recognised qualifications available.

Repairs are usually described as either 'day to day', 'cyclical' or 'major works'.

DAY-TO-DAY REPAIRS

These routine repairs will not usually need a technical expert to work out what needs to be done. Examples would be central heating problems – usually dealt with direct by a qualified engineer – a slipped roof slate or a faulty lock. Often a surveyor will only be called in to carry out inspections on a percentage of the completed jobs, just to check that the repair work has been well done.

CYCLICAL WORK

In order to keep a property weather tight over the years landlords are well advised to redecorate the outside of the house every five years. Other routine tasks can be done at the same time, for example checking the pointing, (the mortar between the bricks): making sure gutters aren't clogged with leaves; seeing that locks, doors and windows are easy to open and close; checking that the paving of any paths, and any fencing or walls around the property, are in good condition.

Surveyors will usually be involved in drawing up what is called the 'specification', describing the work that needs to be done. They will ask various contractors to give a price for doing the job. This is called 'tendering'. Then they will appoint a firm – usually the one offering the lowest price – to do the work. A contract will be drawn up and a timetable agreed and the surveyor will oversee the work.

It is a skilled job to work out what needs to be done at 'cyclical' time. It makes sense to group properties together for economies of scale, especially if scaffolding is to be used. On the other hand there is little point in doing equal amounts of repainting if some properties are showing less signs of wear and tear than others.

There is also a special skill involved in liaising with residents whenever contractors are working on their property. People like to be involved in choosing things such as colour schemes, but sometimes there are conflicting preferences. Inevitably things sometimes go wrong – window panes can get broken by scaffolding; windows may be painted shut; parts of a house can be overlooked. The surveyor in charge therefore needs to be good at explaining what is being done and be tactful and courteous, often acting as an intermediary between the tenant, the contractor and the landlord, who, after all, is paying the bills.

MAJOR REPAIRS AND IMPROVEMENTS

Surveyors are key players when it comes to significant repairs. All components on a property have a natural 'life'. Electrical wiring becomes out of date; plasterwork gets damaged; mortar fails, letting dampness in;

kitchen units fall apart; roofs start to sag and slates and tiles crack. It does not always make sense to go on patching up piecemeal.

Diagnosis is a highly complex job. Anyone can see that a wall is damp, but it takes a person with skill, knowledge and experience to work out whether this is due to rising damp, condensation or damp penetrating from outside, or a leak. In each case the cure will be different. Professionally qualified staff will almost always be in charge of maintenance teams, but there are often posts for trainees who want to qualify or for people who have started work in the building industry but want to move across.

Major works will mean drawing up a plan of repairs that will cost thousands of pounds, and often be carried out on a whole block of flats or an entire estate in one go.

Sometimes major work of this nature will be supervised by outside firms of surveyors or architects, particularly if a large amount of rebuilding or internal remodelling is required. Larger organisations may have an in-house team to do this kind of work. In-house surveyors will work on identifying which properties should be included for a programme of major repairs. They are likely to work closely with the finance and development teams in getting the money approved to pay for the work. They will certainly be a focal point for local residents who should get the chance of being involved with planning the work and choosing some of the improvements – such as the type of kitchen units and what colour front doors will be painted.

INSURANCE CLAIMS

All landlords will be covered by insurance for damage to their buildings. Some insurance claims are easy to deal with, for example if the wind blows a chimney off, or a tree falls and breaks a window. Most claims though are extremely complicated. A crack may appear in the wall of a house that might be due to the soil underneath expanding or contracting; or it might be that the property was badly built and has inadequate foundations.

The cause of damage is often unclear so surveyors will spend a lot of time in discussion with the 'loss adjusters' at the insurance company, deciding what the cause of the problem is, what the cure is, and who's responsible for meeting the cost.

Skills and qualities

Surveyors will usually be qualified through the Royal Institute of Chartered Surveyors or through the Chartered Institute of Building. Many work for private companies, but most local authorities and housing associations employ at least some of their own surveyors directly.

Sometimes support will be given for trainees to qualify while they are at work, through day or block release.

The sorts of qualities needed in someone who will enjoy surveying are:

- a practical interest in how buildings are put together;
- good diagnostic and analytical skills;
- thorough and methodical ways of working;
- pleasure in being outside in all weathers;
- being able to communicate well with all sorts of people;
- a desire to see things through to the very end;
- ability to get work done through others.

Surveyors can't afford to be squeamish: much of their work is to do with drains and gutters and broken loos ... On the other hand good surveyors are worth their weight in gold, both to their employers and to the people who live in the homes they look after.

A day in the life of a maintenance surveyor

8am   Why does it always rain on Fridays? I'll just finish off that specification for the void property I inspected yesterday before I venture out.

9.30am   Can't put it off any longer. I'm meeting one of the housing officers to look at a flat where the tenant has been complaining of damp. Once inside we're quite shocked at how bad it is. There's black mould on the walls of her living room. I take readings, check the ventilation, look outside to see if there are any obvious leaking downpipes or gutters. It's most probably bad condensation, but it's

---

hard to be sure. We ask her about how she heats and airs the flat. You have to be very tactful, but she may not realise that sometimes the way you live affects the dampness in the property.

I promise to go and draw up a solution to the problem, but I warn her this may be just part of the answer. Dampness is notoriously hard to solve. The housing officer asks whether I think the family should be moved out. The child has asthma apparently. We agree to try with fixed ventilation and making sure the place is heated properly, then think again.

10.30am A contractor's coming in to see me. There's been a real problem with tenants complaining his workmen don't turn up on time and are hard to communicate with. It turns out he's got a real problem finding skilled joiners and he's been taking on migrant workers. He says there's too much competition in the industry so he can't afford to pay his workmen much, but swears these guys are really good at what they do. He agrees to make sure that his office tells the men exactly where their appointments are and when, and gives them numbers to ring if there are any language problems on site.

11.30am Weekly voids meeting. We sit down with housing management and update them on all the repairs due on empty flats and when the target date is for the place to be ready for reletting. They blame our contractors for being slow, so we try and get early warning of when tenants are to move out. Trouble is you can't really tell what needs doing until the furniture has all gone and the flat is empty. The meetings are a laugh, usually, as we always try to see who gets their end of the work done quickest, us or the lettings team.

Lunch I go down the road for a sandwich, sharing an umbrella with one of the finance team who processes my contractors' payments. It'd help if we could get them done quicker. Small contractors are always on a knife-edge with their cash flow.

2pm   Tender opening for the cyclical contract on one of our big estates. We have to follow very careful procedures to make sure there's no collusion on pricing. To my surprise the lowest tenderer comes in within £1000 of my estimate. I must be getting better. Or maybe it's luck.

All afternoon I clear my my emails, do my ring-backs, then get stuck into my monthly report for committee. I hear from one of the environmental health people at the council that they're going to give us a grant to put better sound insulation in between two of our flats in a converted house. That's great news.

Nice to get clear before the weekend for once. And we're all going down the pub later because someone's leaving. And it's stopped raining. It **is** my lucky day.

Chapter 4
TENANT INVOLVEMENT AND COMMUNITY DEVELOPMENT

TENANT INVOLVEMENT

There has been a major shift in the relationship between tenant and landlord over the last 20 years. As in the commercial sector, tenants are now viewed as 'customers'. Through paying their rent they are buying a standard of service and can influence the way in which that service is provided.

Tenants play a positive and constructive role in making sure work is done efficiently and well. There are different degrees of involvement:

Information

At the most basic level, there is a statutory duty to make varous kinds of information openly available to tenants Most housing organisations will go well beyond this, by publicising information about their policies, practices and procedures through newsletters, annual reports, circulars, on their website, in local papers, on radio and so on. This is integral to good customer relations.

Consultation

Tenants have a legal right through their tenancy agreement to be consulted about changes that affect them. Consultation might be done via a questionnaire, through an open meeting or by letter. For example, if a housing association decides to stop receiving rent payments at a local office it would have to ask the tenants who use that facility what they think about the proposed change. The landlord would have to take into account what tenants say, but still has the right to decide to go ahead with the change.

Involvement

Involving tenants and local people implies a closer working relationship, perhaps through tenants' associations on estates. The tenants' association might work very closely with a landlord when for example major refurbishment work is being done on an estate. Tenants might be involved in planning the sequence of work, what kind of paint colours are chosen and what fixtures and fittings are selected. Public landlords work to fixed budgets and tenants will often be asked to help prioritise where the money should be spent.

Participation

While some residents only want to be asked about matters that affect them directly others may want to make a wider impact. Committees of housing associations will now usually have at least some tenant members. They may be elected by other tenants or they may put their own names forward. Each association is different.

Decision-making structures are changing but housing committees at local authorities may co-opt tenants – that is, ask tenant representatives to serve on the committee in order to make sure that tenants' views are taken into account and that they can play a genuine part in decision-making. In the LSVT associations tenants will be in the lead. Many associations have tenants making up one third of their committee membership. Committees will be responsible for policy and for deciding matters such as the level of annual rent increases.

Control

There are many ways in which tenants can take complete control of how their homes are managed. In a cooperative, for example, the management committee will be made up entirely of tenants, who will take all the decisions. Arm's length management organisations, tenant management organisations and other new types of organisation put tenants at the front.

Community Development

Many landlords now want to play a much wider part in helping the neighbourhoods they work in become better places to live. The changing industrial base of the country has led to economic decline in some regions. There is a higher proportion of unemployed and low-income households living in social rented housing than there is amongst the population as a whole.

A combination of factors can lead to the collapse of the local economy. Local authorities and housing associations may be the largest landlords in some of the more deprived communities and are well placed to use their resources for the wider benefit of the people who live in their homes. Residents may not have had the chance to develop their skills and capacities. Housing associations, for example, can make links with local schools, colleges and employers to create opportunities for local people, helping them into jobs.

WHAT DO TENANT PARTICIPATION AND COMMUNITY DEVELOPMENT WORKERS DO?

Many large landlords now employ staff who work with local residents, enabling them to develop the skills and abilities to improve the neighbourhoods they live in themselves. Tenant participation work will encourage people to get involved, setting up informal and formal tenants' networks.

Community development work means getting to know what people's concerns and problems are and helping them find ways to resolve those problems. The contacts and influence of the landlord can be very useful. For example, a tenants' association may be concerned about the lack of facilities for young people on their estate. The community development worker will work with them to identify what is wanted, might help with fund-raising and will help the tenants group make the right connections. Arranging training for tenants is an increasingly important part of the work, equipping them with the skills they need, especially where they are involved in big regeneration projects.

Skills and qualities
Effective tenant participation workers will be good communicators who can encourage other people to develop their talents and abilities. They must want to enable people to do things for themselves. They have to be

diplomatic and patient: real lasting change can take a long time to bring about.

A day in the life of a tenant participation worker

The trouble with my job is no one really understands what I do. Last night I was out late at a tenants' meeting on an estate. My employers want to see tenants' associations set up everywhere. The idea is great, but to start with people are either more concerned with other things going on in their lives or just suspicious. Sometimes, like last night, they were simply angry because there's a long-running saga about rotten window frames in the flats and that's all they wanted to talk about. Well, did they shout at me about it to start with! Still, everyone calmed down eventually and I can't blame them; from their point of view the windows must be number one priority.

But my aim is to help people to take charge of what goes on in their patch. This means helping them to organise themselves, unearthing talent, trying to encourage people to negotiate what's negotiable rather than just complain. Luckily I can take a long-term view. I used to work for a council that worked with its tenants and eventually had a vote to transfer all the properties into a new organisation which could release money for the repairs that were needed. Tenants took charge there in the long run but it took a while. I must be patient.

Anyway, I arranged with one of the women at the meeting that I'd pop down and see her today. She was too shy to speak up at the meeting. Went to her flat as arranged. She said there are a number of them who would like to get involved in something practical for the children on the estate. This sounds like a good way in to me. We talked about all the different sources of money available, from the Lottery to Europe. We think we're going to go for a Community Training and Enabling Grant from the Housing Corporation if there might be training for tenants wanting to get skills and qualifications in childcare out of it.

I agree to get one of the community workers from the council to talk with her group about what the children might need. After a bit of nervousness she agrees that she'll put a proposal up to the next tenants' meeting if I'll help her rehearse what she has to say. She's interested in finding out about local courses now her children are both at school. She says her confidence is pretty low, having been at home with them as toddlers, and having left school with no qualifications. She seems really sparky to me, and I'll do whatever she thinks I can to help.

During the afternoon I'm writing a 'tenant participation strategy' to discuss with the tenant services director at my next supervision, when she goes through my work with me and we prioritise what I need to do next month. Specially important in a job like mine, which can be as big as I want it to be. She didn't think much of my first stab at it. But she helped me to understand what the shape of a committee paper ought to be, with recommendations and everything. We're looking at lots of different ways for people to get involved, from local events, through helping with our customer services training, to standing for election to our committee.

It's quite hard for some staff to get used to me putting the tenants' viewpoint all the time. But they are our customers and they know what goes on out there. We would do well to listen to what they tell us.

No evening meeting tonight but I'll go past the college and drop those brochures about courses off. Next time she can go herself, but it's hard to get someone to look after the kids when you're on your own with no money for babysitters and you don't like asking favours. If she takes up studying she'll soon be back to work herself, I'll bet.

Chapter 5
HOMELESSNESS

INTRODUCTION

Thousands of people become homeless every year. This may be because a private tenancy is brought to an end and they have no alternative place to go; it may be because a family splits up; it might be that domestic violence means children have to be housed elsewhere. In all parts of the country, especially London and the south-east, there are refugees and asylum seekers who have arrived with nowhere to go.

Local authorities have a statutory duty to advise people who become homeless of how they can secure housing (although the law is changing) – and they must offer housing if children, older people or vulnerable people are involved.

Local authorities, especially those in the big conurbations, will have teams set up just to help homeless families and individuals, where each person's case and prospects are carefully examined and solutions found. Sometimes, especially in the case of families with children, temporary accommodation in bed and breakfast hotels or hostels, paid for by the local authority, is the only answer, as the kind of permanent property the family needs may not be available immediately.

Working with homeless families is extremely tough. The human predicament is hard to deal with when the kind of homes people want to live in are often just not available. This is particularly true in London and the south-east, where housing is expensive and demand for it is intense.

Staff in homeless families teams will often have a difficult job in establishing exactly what the applicant's history and entitlement is, especially if the applicant does not communicate easily in English. Staff will need to have good knowledge of the legislation and understand what applicants are entitled to. They will need to do a lot of liaison with other local authority departments, such as environmental health and social services. They will liaise with government agencies and sometimes the police and probation service. Assessing applicants' cases is hard and takes time. Staff need to be thorough and patient, but meanwhile be able to cope with the wishes and anxieties of the person who has nowhere to go.

Working in homelessness is the true sharp end of housing. But it offers insights into the real importance of housing as a profession. It was the increase in awareness of homelessness in the 1960s that brought the pressure group Shelter to the fore, and Shelter, with others, promoted the growth of housing associations to help solve the shortage of housing that people could afford.

Shelter

Campaigning, projects and housing aid and advice

Shelter offers:

Practical help

- over 50 Housing Aid Centres and Projects providing expert information, advice and advocacy to over 100,000 people a year in England and Scotland;
- Shelterline, a free, national helpline providing advice and information 24 hours a day, 365 days a year;
- five Homeless to Home Projects, piloting ways of resettling families who have experienced homelessness into new accommodation;
- the Street Homelessness Project, working with local authorities and other voluntary organisations to develop local strategies for reducing rough sleeping;
- the National Homelessness Advice Service, providing secondary advice to all Citizens Advice Bureaux;
- the new Homework Project, which seeks to prevent homelessness by providing information and education materials for young people in school.

Shelter also campaigns, and offers training

More information at www.shelter.org.uk

TEMPORARY ACCOMMODATION AND PRIVATE SECTOR LEASING

As bed and breakfast type and hostel accommodation is not a satisfactory solution for homeless families, especially for the children, many alternative ways of offering short-term solutions have been found.

Some housing associations take leases on privately owned property for say three or five-year terms and act as their managing agents. They then agree with the local authority to offer these flats on a furnished and temporary basis to families who are homeless and whose cases are being assessed. This is particularly useful for asylum seekers, where the assessment may take some time.

Managing temporary accommodation is a highly skilled job – the people housed are likely to be vulnerable and need a lot of support during this transitional period while they are waiting to hear what the final outcome of their application will be. At the same time the private landlord who owns the property wants to be sure that his or her property is well maintained, and that the rent will be paid promptly.

STREET HOMELESSNESS AND 'ROUGH SLEEPING'

One of the high-profile aspects of housing is the number of people who sleep on the street, either because they have no alternative or through choice.

There are a number of voluntary organisations working with street homeless people. Night shelters and hostels offer respite. There are also organisations that specialise in helping 'resettle' people who have been used to sleeping rough.

Often finding someone a place to live is only part of the solution: people who have lived on the street may have other difficulties – health or drug or alcohol problems, no job prospects – or simply find it hard to adjust to the loneliness that a flat of your own can bring.

Young people who are homeless are particularly vulnerable, and organisations such as Centrepoint in London are there to help not just with housing but with helping young people to find training and work and develop the life skills they need in order to flourish independently.

Skills and qualities

As with housing management work, you'll have a real desire to help people who are going through traumatic times and often have intractable problems. You'll need to be resourceful. A combination of empathy, objectivity and energy will help you to help clients find solutions to their housing problems. And of course an understanding of the legislation and the work of other agencies who can help will be essential.

Chapter 6
OTHER KINDS OF ACCOMMODATION

KEY WORKERS AND STUDENT ACCOMMODATION

A growing market in rented housing is that for 'key workers' and for students. Rental and home purchase prices in many areas, especially London and the south-east, have shot well outside the means of people on low or average incomes.

Nurses, for example, may need to live near their place of work, especially as they work anti-social hours, so cannot easily commute to places where housing is cheaper. Hospitals are transferring their staff accommodation to housing organisations who will modernise it and manage it to a high standard. Sometimes housing organisations act as managing agents. Or they may take a lease on the property or purchase it outright.

The same goes for student housing. Universities and colleges are transferring the management and sometimes the ownership of their student hostels to professional managing bodies. Managing student housing is a discipline on its own. Instead of living in fully self-contained flats students are likely to have bed-sits where they share kitchens, common rooms and sometimes bathrooms with others. Students only need their housing during term-time and are likely to go back home in the holidays. But the landlords need to have rent coming in all year round in order to be able to pay for repairs and renewals, and to repay the money they will have borrowed for the cost of building or refurbishing the accommodation.

This demands a different style of management from the other kinds of housing discussed in Chapters 1 and 2. But, as we have seen throughout this book, the skills and competencies you acquire if you start off running student housing will be transferable to other sectors, and just as valid if you decide you want to train for a professional qualification.

PRIVATE LANDLORDS

In the UK there are many people who rent their homes from a private landlord. Most are 'small landlords' – people who own just one or two properties that they rent out. Some are large landlords, such as the Crown, the Church Commissioners and the old aristocratic estates such as Grosvenor, Cadogan and de Walden in London, which have large commercial as well as residential holdings.

There are plenty of opportunities in housing management positions here as well. The Association of Residential Management Agents and Association of Residential Letting Agents can give you information about the likely scope of jobs and what experience would be useful. The two main differences between private sector and public sector landlords is that the private sector landlord has more control over who to select to be a tenant and is less likely to offer subsidised rents and the legislation for leasehold management and the style is different.

SHARED OWNERSHIP AND LEASEHOLD MANAGEMENT

In this sector too changes abound. Where people own a long lease on flats in a house or blocks of flats, someone has to be responsible for the painting and decoration of the shared parts of the property, such as the hall and stairways, and for repairs to roofs and lifts. Joint management or service companies are being set up to do this work and there is a growing need for efficient operators in this expanding market.

Over the last 20 years many council and housing association flats and houses have been sold to sitting tenants under the 'Right to Buy' scheme. There are also a number of different arrangements that help people with low incomes get their feet on the ladder of being home owners. So landlords are often responsible for managing estates or individual properties where some residents are tenants and some own – or part own – their homes.

Managing properties where people have different responsibilities and interests is particularly challenging. People who have a direct personal interest in the value of the property because they own it and may wish to sell their interest on are likely to be especially keen to see their home well maintained and the environment around it well kept. Friction can easily develop between neighbours who have different interests in how their properties are run, and people with a financial stake in their housing may have higher expectations of the service they get from their landlord – that is, the freehold owner of the property – than people who are renting.

Housing associations that offer shared ownership housing will also be involved in the marketing of new schemes for sale and the selling on of properties when owners move on. If the sales and estate agency side of housing appeals to you then you could get valuable experience in shared ownership.

Skills and qualities
As with the jobs described earlier you'll need to be super-efficient, well organised and able to cope with a demanding clientele. You'll find real transferability of your experience between the commercial world of estate agencies and private management agencies.

Chapter 7
CARE, SUPPORT, ADVICE AND BENEFIT WORK

Many tenants need care and support because of ill health or other disadvantage. Many housing associations were set up specifically to work with groups who have special needs – not just somewhere to live, but help to run their lives day to day.

This might include:

- elderly people who are physically or mentally frail;
- people with mental ill health;
- young people who have grown up in institutional care;
- people who use drugs or alcohol;
- adults with learning difficulties.

The extent of specialist training and the qualifications needed by people wanting to work in care is outside the scope of this book. However, it is worth being aware that councils and associations often work closely with voluntary organisations who specialise in the care and support of vulnerable people. Some councils and associations also employ care workers directly, especially those who work with elderly people who live in residential or 'care' homes, where 24-hour help, including meals, is provided.

If you are working as a carer in, say, a residential home, it is worth remembering that housing associations as well as local authorities may also have job offers available from time to time. A lot of people transfer from one sector to another. Hourly pay rates may not be very high, so other factors such as level of job satisfaction, journey to work, general terms and conditions (including training offered) may be things to think about especially carefully.

A significant number of people moving into ordinary council or housing association properties who do not need full-time care do still have difficulties that are beyond the expertise of staff who are trained in housing management. For example, they may have mental ill health, face language and cultural barriers or lack knowledge about the availability of both financial and social support. Although housing officers will always have some contact with social workers, the health services and the police and probation service, it is quite a specialist task to coordinate support for people who cannot otherwise live independently.

Associations and councils will often employ staff with special expertise to help vulnerable tenants to cope and to make sure that appropriate 'care packages' are in place and working.

Skills and qualities for working in care

You'll need to have a real empathy with your clients, who may be very frail; at the same time you need to be able not to get too personally involved. You must be practical and good at working with other people – teamwork matters a great deal in care. You need to have respect for all your clients, a desire to help them keep their independence as far as possible and an enthusiasm for training; a cheerful and patient outlook on life is likely to be appreciated.

BENEFITS ADVICE

The welfare benefit system is also extremely complicated and many people, particularly older people, do not claim all the benefits they are entitled to. As well as housing benefit and old age pensions there may be a range of disability entitlements that people don't know about, or think they are not eligible for. They may therefore be poorer than they need be, with all the disadvantage that brings in terms of health and well-being. People whose work or family patterns change will also find that the benefits they are entitled to change as well, and this may affect their ability to pay the rent.

There are many specialist positions in benefits advice, and much of the knowledge of people working in employment, social security or Inland Revenue offices is transferable to advisory posts in housing organisations. There are not large numbers of such specialist advice jobs available in housing organisations. It is more likely that you would start your career off in a government department or at a council, perhaps in administering housing benefit.

GENERAL ADVICE AND HOUSING AID WORK

Offices such as the Citizens Advice Bureaux receive a number of housing-based enquiries. Voluntary advice work with a CAB or independent advice centre can be a pathway into this kind of work, homelessness, housing advice and housing generally. Some cities support the specialised work of independent aid and advice agencies that help individuals with their housing problems. This could include helping tenants facing eviction, or working with the environmental health department of the local council on health and safety matters, or countering poor practice from a landlord.

The legislation and the regulations are immensely complicated and change frequently. Organisations that employ advisers, whether on benefits or on general housing problems, must be sure that thorough and regular training is given to ensure that advice is of the best possible quality.

Skills and qualities

You are likely to be good at this kind of work if you are interested in legal matters and the question of rights, accurate with figures, clear at explaining complicated things in a straightforward way to people who will not know all the jargon, and like to get things right. In general advice work you will find it useful to be a good networker and to have good knowledge of locally available resources for different clients, such as voluntary organisations or charities that can give help to special needs groups.

Chapter 8
LIVING ON THE JOB

CARETAKERS AND WARDENS

Landlords often employ local estate managers, or neighbourhood wardens (or supercaretakers). Under the new neighbourhood management proposals these kinds of jobs will become more interesting and will have more authority and power to deal with problems on the ground. Caretakers often live as tenants on the estate they look after. Their jobs may include a range of essential day-to-day practical functions, such as:

- keeping common halls and stairways clean and tidy;
- changing light bulbs in communal lighting;
- supervising gardening and grass-cutting;
- sweeping paths;
- ensuring that bin and park areas are well kept;
- sometimes arranging repairs, or doing basic 'handyman' jobs as required;
- keeping an eye out for any anti-social or criminal behaviour.

Usually caretakers will live rent free or with a reduced rent.

The government is keen to see better management provided at neighbourhood level, and there are many opportunities now for a wider role; this might include liaising with the police where there are problems of anti-social behaviour on estates, such as drug dealing.

Caretakers and local estate managers play a vital role as far as tenants are concerned in keeping estates looking and feeling clean and well cared for.

The same goes for wardens in 'sheltered schemes'. These are blocks of flats or bungalows designed for people over retirement age, or people with disabilities, where a warden is available to offer basic help, as a good neighbour might, to people as they become more frail. Some sheltered schemes now use the cheaper option of linking in to a 24-hour central call system – so that an elderly person can get help at any time – but wardens continue to offer a real service.

Modern Apprenticeships

You can earn money while working in a housing job by becoming a Modern Apprentice. If you want to go straight into a job, not study full-time anymore, this could help you get qualifications on the way. Details are available through your local Learning and Skills Council or Housing Potential UK.

HOSTEL STAFF – SUPPORTED HOUSING

A number of councils and housing associations offer supported 'shared housing' to people who prefer not to or are unable to live alone. An example would be a house available for young people leaving local authority care or with learning difficulties who would need help learning to budget, shop, cook, clean, pay bills and so on.

Usually each resident would have their own bedroom and would share the kitchen and living room. Often there is a paid member of staff who lives in, and whose job is to help the residents with their day-to-day affairs. Sometimes these staff are employed directly by the landlord, but more often a specialist voluntary organisation will be responsible for deciding who moves into the house and who the house warden is. There are many different titles used for describing these positions – 'support worker', 'warden', 'hostel worker', 'support tenant', 'house-parent' and so on. There are also many 'floating support schemes' where the help goes with the individual (rather than the house where they live). If this sort of work appeals to you (whether living in or out), then it would be worth contacting the local or the national office of the relevant voluntary organisations. The National Council for Voluntary Organisations can give contact details. Here are some charities which have housing projects:

- Scope, which works with people with cerebral palsy;
- Mencap, which works with people with learning difficulties;
- RNIB (The Royal National Institute for the Blind);
- RNID (The Royal National Institute for Deaf People);

- Mind, which works to promote mental health;
- Sense, which works with people who are sensorily impaired, usually through blindness and deafness;
- The Abbeyfields Societies, which provide for older single people who prefer not to live alone.

Addresses for these and other similar organisations are at the back of the book.

If you think you might be interested in a career working with people with support needs but are not sure, you might want to do some voluntary work first. Any of the above organisations could tell you what opportunities there are where you live. You may have a Volunteer Bureau or local Council for Voluntary Service.

Help the Aged, Age Concern and the Alzheimer's Society will be able to give you guidance about work opportunities with older people. Their addresses are at the back of the book.

Skills and qualities

Being practical, full of common sense and having a sense of humour are good qualities for caretakers and wardens, as much as for anyone involved in care. Empathy, a real desire to help other people, reliability and patience are all helpful qualities to have.

In care, training and qualifications will vary, but there is a wide range of qualifications available , and this might also be a useful background if you were thinking of moving into a career in social work eventually.

Chapter 9
OTHER KINDS OF WORK

INTRODUCTION

All housing organisations employ staff who are trained in disciplines
quite different from housing management, from accountancy to
architecture. If you were aiming for a career in another discipline it
would still be worth thinking about the benefits of applying your
technical and professional skills within the non-profit sector.

REGENERATION AND DEVELOPMENT

Much exciting work is being done to bring back life into run-down areas.
Housing associations are involved in huge investment programmes,
working side by side with major commercial investors. From Salford
Docks to the Dome you will find housing development staff involved
with planning how to put new and attractive but affordable rented
housing in alongside the renovated industrial buildings and the shops and
commercial centres.

The larger housing associations have development teams whose job it is
to purchase land for building new homes, to buy homes that need
refurbishing or to work with other organisations such as local authorities
on the large-scale regeneration of run-down central city areas.
Development teams will be responsible for ensuring that the way in
which land is bought and homes built ('procured') is done strictly in
accordance with all the guidelines laid down by the government through
the Housing Corporation in England.

As housing associations use a lot of public money for their work what they
do is strictly controlled. Costs have to be kept down but the quality of what
is built is very high. Associations have to be sure that their properties are of
a decent space standard, and built to high standards of energy efficiency.

The development team will probably include people whose background is in surveying, architecture and administration. They will normally work with private firms of architects and private building contractors, and they will project manage the whole building scheme – from the purchase of the land, through the design stage, planning and seeing the building work is done to timetable and to budget. It is worth remembering how varied the work of different associations is. Some work in rural areas, where there may be just as much challenge in building a handful of cottages in keeping with the long-established local style of building using local materials as there would be in putting up a new estate.

Smaller associations may 'contract out' their development work, using a larger association's staff to do it for them.

Development staff often get good opportunities to move from one employer to another and will find their skills and experience as useful in a private development company as in a non-profit organisation.

CASE STUDY

Joseph Ogbonna tells his own story

Born 1962 Studied to first degree level in Nigeria. First degree in Psychology (Hons) 2.1 in 1984. Came to live in UK in 1991 with working experience of aptitude testing and construction project management.

Nov 1991 Worked for then Dept of Environment as administrative assistant in the Housing Registry. Repossessions were rife and LSVT associations had recently been introduced. Registered and filed appeals from ordinary people to government to intervene in individual repossession cases and local authority applications for consent passed through the Registry. They were interesting and I developed an interest in housing.

Aug 1992 Started training with PATH London (see below) and posted to William Sutton Trust in Tring. Specific skills training and monitoring by PATH was crucial to job success. Placements within The William Sutton Trust included estates management positions in London and Hemel Hempstead, development, technical services, housing policy, allocations and lettings, finance. Exposure to various aspects of housing at an early stage enabled an understanding of my role and linkages between various services.

Aug 1993 First full-time position as housing officer (special needs) at London and Quadrant – achieved BTec HNC (Housing) and CIH Test of Professional Practice (TPP1) and started TPP2. Driven by a belief that career progress would be supported by a combination of experience and qualifications.

July 1995 Started six-month secondment to special needs development and progressed to permanent role as development officer. Completed CIH TPP2 module. Exposure to wide variety of own and colleagues' development schemes including general needs, special needs, student accommodation, health authority schemes.

Sept 1996 Started MBA (Executive) programme – hard work with employment and a young family.

Feb 1997 Started employment with Octavia Hill Housing Trust as senior development officer, later senior project manager. Responsible for various new-build, refurbishment and major repairs schemes. Learnt valuable lessons in applying a customer focus to development and its impact on successful operation of a housing association. Timely for the introduction of Best Value in 1999. Completed MBA programme with emphasis on strategic management.

Feb 2000 Business improvement manager, responsible for initiatives to improve business processes and outputs including Best Value in Family Housing Association. Increased opportunities to utilise business training. Consolidating project management experience.

View that housing could provide a varied and rewarding career but progress requires hard work, investment in self-development and active management of own career. All this in an ever-changing environment.

PATH (Positive Action for Training in Housing)

PATH National is a skills development agency that aims to increase the employability and leadership qualities of black and ethnic minority people.

They offer two main programmes, for new entrants to the sector (traineeship programme) and for existing housing sector employees (fast-track management development programme).

For more information contact:
Research and Development Officer

PATH National Ltd
Whittington House
London N19 3JG
tel: 020 7281 8001
email: pranade@pathuk.co.uk

POLICY AND RESEARCH

Larger housing organisations, especially local authorities, need to spend a lot of time thinking about and planning how they will run their services to meet ever-changing needs and to help bring about continuous improvement. Research and analysis has become central to the way housing organisations operate, playing a real practical role in helping to find ways of doing things better.

All housing associations and councils have to keep very detailed records and statistics of everything they do and report both to their own committees, councillors and also, ultimately, to the government. These statistics, called 'performance indicators', help the managers and customers to judge how well they are performing compared to other similar landlords, and that means having to ask themselves whether a different way of working might deliver better results.

Under a system known as 'Best Value' public landlords have to compare both the quality and the cost of what they do and ask their customers what they think of the service too. So research, often through customer satisfaction surveys, interviews and focus groups, is vitally important and has a very direct and useful result. The emphasis is on finding better ways of doing things.

It is very useful for managers to look at their performance statistics regularly. This will highlight problems that arise, for example rent arrears may start to go up. This could indicate that there are difficulties with the local housing benefit office which need to be sorted out. Performance statistics might show that while some repairs are always done on time others are not, and this might mean that a particular maintenance contractor is not working efficiently.

Sometimes the information presented in the statistics will lead to the need to review a particular policy. In some parts of the country some kinds of property have become difficult to find tenants for. The statistics will show how long it takes to let vacant homes in different locations. If the statistics start to show that an estate or a street has begun to become undesirable managers will need to see whether the 'lettings policy' for the area needs changing. For example, an estate might have a large number of families with children, but may not have good facilities for them. It may be necessary for the landlord both to work with the community to improve what's there for children and also to talk to the local council and get agreement to letting future vacancies to people without children.

Staff working in policy, research and information play a vital role in helping their organisation continue to meet housing needs in the most effective way. Research and policy skills are 'generic' in the sense that they can be applied to any subject – not just housing. Moreover, research jobs in local authorities and housing associations can lead to wide varieties of work for colleges and universities, independent research institutions, or trade associations such as the National Housing Federation, professional bodies such as the CIH and for local or national government associations.

PUBLIC RELATIONS AND FUND-RAISING

'Social' housing organisations do not always have a very good image – or, more likely, they may not be known about at all. It is important that their work is known and understood, not just within their own communities but in the wider world.

Staff who work in public relations will have a range of jobs. They are likely to be responsible for publications – such as tenant newsletters, annual reports, articles in the trade press and events – such as the openings of new buildings, the annual general meeting, and staff conferences. Often they will be responsible for fund-raising for special activities.

Skills and qualities
People who enjoy public relations work are usually sociable and creative, with a good eye for detail and an awareness of the wider political context. They can usually write in a range of styles depending on the target audience and the purpose, for example journalistic flair for a

tenants' newletter, a more polished approach for corporate brochures or annual reports.

MARKETING

Housing associations compete vigorously in all sorts of ways – for government money to build new homes, for local authority support for city regeneration projects, for contracts to provide care to vulnerable people – these are just some examples. Large associations will employ staff whose skills are in 'selling' what their organisation can do. This is highly competitive and is a growth area, with a fairly commercial approach. Many regions of the country have literally hundreds of associations. The marketing staff help explain to funders what special qualities their association can offer. This helps funders decide which will be the best one to work with on a particular scheme – ultimately who will get the work and the money to go with it.

FINANCE

Finance departments think they are the hub of any organisation. In housing organisations they have the huge task of keeping control of and recording the money coming in – from rents, from government grants and from private loans.

Equally they keep control of the money going out – which will range from cheques for hundreds of thousands of pounds to contractors for monthly payments for building work, through paying salaries to handling the petty cash.

A large finance team will include people who are professionally qualified as accountants as well as those who are studying for management accountancy or bookkeeping and basic accounting qualifications.

The finance team will be involved in preparing the organisation's annual plan and budget, as well as forecasting financial viability for the next 5–15 years or more. Senior staff will be responsible for raising loans from private investors for new construction work and also obtaining approval for grants. They will do what is called 'treasury management' making sure that money is well invested. Because public money is used for building it is very important that the financial affairs of local authorities and housing associations are run properly.

'Risk management' is a big part of the responsibility. This means making sure that no excessive risks are taken, especially on new schemes, that could damage the viability of the organisation.

Careful auditing is very important too, not just to make sure that the books are straight at the end of the year, but that good systems and controls over the flow of money are properly run, for the sake of efficiency and to minimise the risk of fraud. Annual audits are normally carried out by external firms of qualified auditors. The Housing Corporation also inspects and regulates the full range of housing association work. The Audit Commission inspects local authorities.

Calculating the annual rent charged for each property is a complicated task, as there are new controls and guidance from government tending to keep rent increases down, while at the same time housing organisations must have enough money coming in to do repairs, repay loans, pay the staff and invest in new work.

Finance teams are always especially busy at the end of the financial year when external auditors come in to check that all the money coming in and going out has been properly accounted for. Finance teams will be in charge of internal controls – making sure that there are proper procedures and authorities in place and enough cross-checking to make sure that there is no scope for fraud, or for inefficiency in the running of the organisation's affairs.

Many finance staff will have the job of ensuring that money due comes in at the right time. This could include rent from tenants, claiming government grants and collecting payments due from local councils.

Skills and Qualities
Good finance staff are likely to:

- be good at coping with routine;
- enjoy seeing things through to the end;

- be ordered and methodical in their approach to problem solving;
- be good at figure work.

INFORMATION TECHNOLOGY

Some exciting and innovative work is going on in using technology to improve services for tenants. For example, experiments for tenants being able to diagnose and report repairs online; paying rent by swipe card is available to tenants of some larger landlords; staff out on site can take laptops to help give benefit and welfare advice; development teams bid for allocations of government money online; annual returns are also dealt with electronically. In local authorities there will be an IT department that services the housing staff – carrying out upgrades, training and troubleshooting, developing new software for systems and so on. In small organisations the 'IT department' might be just one person, who will usually have learned the technical skills elsewhere. Hardware and software packages may be supplied by external contractors, in which case the IT people need to be very good at interpreting the jargon and translating what the housing staff want into language the techies can understand! The government wants all services to be available online by 2005, so IT is a real growth area for careers in housing.

Skills and Qualities

In addition to the obvious technical abilities, good communication skills and a calm approach to problem-solving make IT staff some of the most in demand of all.

HUMAN RESOURCES

Some housing organisations are now very big employers indeed, with upwards of 1000 staff. Even those with only 20 or 30 staff are likely to need quite sophisticated knowledge of employment law. Housing organisations generally aim to be good and fair employers. Personnel teams – or 'human resources' as they are often called – will be responsible for:

- recruitment;
- induction and training;

- personal and career development at work;
- restructuring (that is, implementing changes in the way people have to do their jobs);
- promotions;
- salary and benefits packages;
- union relations;
- appraisal systems;
- grievance and disciplinary problems.

Skills and qualities

Staff in personnel have to be able to keep all manner of confidences. They need to be fair and impartial, efficient at dealing with any problems that staff or managers may bring them (no matter how big or small) and genuinely interested in seeing managers and staff working harmoniously together. No organisation can flourish unless morale is good, and staff in the human resources field are crucial in promoting healthy and constructive relationships at work. Assistants in personnel departments may well train to become qualified through the Chartered Institute of Personal Development.

LEGAL SERVICES

Local authorities and some housing associations will have their own in-house legal teams. They may work on company secretarial matters, conveyancing of land or property, preparing contracts, helping on tenancy problems and so on. Solicitors employed within local government will be professionally qualified and may well have worked in private practice. Most associations appoint private firms to do their legal work.

OFFICE MANAGEMENT

There is one other area of work often overlooked but essential – office management. In any office a breakdown in the operation of day-to-day apparatus causes irritation at best – and meltdown at worst!

Office managers will ensure there is a continuous supply of stationery, that phones and faxes are kept working well, that security is good, that the office cleaners do their work thoroughly, that the health and safety of employees is assured, that staff have what they need to do the job in the practical way of chairs, desks, files and so on.

Office management skills can easily be transferred from one kind of employer to another. Housing organisations often deal with stressed and poor 'customers' and having as welcoming and well functioning an office environment as possible, within limited budgets, is specially important for both visitors and staff. So the office manager has a particularly interesting and challenging role. If the building from which the housing services are offered is in good order and works well customers are more likely to believe that the organisation itself is in good order and works well.

Skills and qualities

Office management jobs are often poorly regarded in terms of pay and status, and many people get their first work experience in a busy post-room – don't throw this experience away: it could be useful if the practical side of making an office tick over well appeals to you. You see everything that goes on, and you will never be out of a job!

OTHER EMPLOYERS

While the general idea of working in housing may appeal to you, but you prefer the idea of getting a broad understanding of the sector before committing yourself to a particular career, you might want to think about working in the Civil Service, the Housing Corporation (which allocates funds to and regulates housing associations) or one of the trade associations such as the National Housing Federation, or one of the tenant empowerment organisations such as the Tenant Participation Advisory Service. If you have a legal background you might feel drawn to the different ombudsman services that handle complaints from members of the public who believe their local authority or housing association has not dealt with their complaint adequately. Although the work of the regulators, mentioned earlier, may be rather specialised, there is a need for applicants. The Housing Corporation has inspectors based in its regional offices. Applicants from black and minority ethnic backgrounds are often in short supply for these posts. And the Housing Inspectorate advertises from time to time for inspectors who are tenants of councils or associations as part of the quality assurance side of inspection. Special training is made available for inspectors.

VOLUNTEERING

One route to finding out more about what housing has to offer could be by serving on the board of a housing association for a while as a volunteer. This might be particularly appropriate if you are someone who already has experience elsewhere, for example in a different profession, but are thinking of transferring into the sector. Or you might be thinking of returning to work after a career break. There are a number of addresses and contact details at the back of this book that may help you to find out more about the possibilities.

CASE STUDY

The story of a woman who came into housing as a mature entrant

Having spent a number of years in the 1980s as a single parent locked in the poverty trap of not being able to earn enough to pay for someone to look after my son while I worked, I grabbed the opportunity as soon as I was able to pursue my education as a mature student.

On leaving university with a qualification in business and finance I had a clear idea of the type of business I wanted to work in, but it wasn't until I began as a temp for a big housing association that I realised the varied career opportunities available in the housing sector.

I began inputting invoices, became the administrator for the HAMA Scheme (Housing Associations as Managing Agents) and have been the project coordinator for the information management and technology department for the past four years. I have been involved in numerous dynamic and exciting projects and now have an extensive skills base in project management.

Master of Business Administration, the MBA

Increasing numbers of people wanting careers as managers and directors in housing organisations are taking their MBAs. The disciplines learned in business administration are just as relevant and

58

applicable to housing, where knowing how to plan and manage a business with a social purpose is, if anything, more complex than one driven by the need to satisfy shareholders alone. Some universities, such as Birmingham, offer courses that can be done part-time alongside work; student Nadhia Hussain, quoted in *Inside Housing*, said, 'I hope to broaden my understanding of how different organisations work. The benefit of studying with individuals from other sectors, for example the police and the health service, is that I can learn more about the challenges facing these sectors in the 21st century. Learn to think outside the "housing box", if you like.'

Chapter 10
WORKING ABROAD

Many other countries are building links with housing managers in the UK. For example there is a branch of the Chartered Institute of Housing in Hong Kong. Public sector housing work is widespread in countries within the Commonwealth, the EU, the USA and elsewhere, and there is a range of private sector agencies fulfilling a variety of management roles. In countries with a federal system of government, such as Australia and Canada, information about work opportunities is to be had from each state's federal government.

If you are thinking about working abroad in housing you would be well advised to contact the relevant Embassies or High Commissions of the countries that interest you to find out the opportunities and names and addresses of organisations which might help. The Chartered Institute of Housing will also be able to make suggestions.

Homeless International

This is a charity whose objectives are:

- to provide financial and technical support to charitable organisations and groups working to improve shelter conditions of the poor in Asia, Africa, Latin America, the Caribbean and Europe;
- to support the international exchange of information and experience on homelessness.

Last year it worked in nine different countries, on 14 projects, affecting 1 million households, providing financial services, organising technical advice, acting as advocates, supporting partners and carrying out research into long-term solutions to poverty.

For more information check its website at www.homeless-international.org

---

PART TWO:
OTHER IMPORTANT FACTORS

Chapter 11
PAY AND PROSPECTS

Never has there been a more exciting time, with so much opportunity, to come into housing. There is massive growth, especially in the housing association sector, and employers want the right mix of skills to deliver new initiatives as well as maintain existing quality of service. Quite a challenge. It's a profession where individual staff can make a real impact early on in their careers. Rented housing in Britain is being transformed and neighbourhoods are being revitalised by all the investment taking place. There's also a shortage of people coming into the sector and a recruitment drive is under way to find people with the talent, energy and commitment to making a real difference to people's lives and to the prospects for their children. Employers now look for competency and potential in applicants, as much as for qualifications.

Housing organisations are great places to work, and some of the reasons are set out in this chapter. It would need a second book to give proper details of pay levels of all the different jobs in housing and how they are decided. And it would need updating every year. But there are annual surveys published that analyse the range of pay levels for jobs in different housing organisations, according to size and location, year by year, and a snapshot for 2002 published in *Inside Housing* in January 2002 for finance jobs is set out in the table on the following page.

LARGE HOUSING ASSOCIATIONS

	Finance director			Part-qualified CIMA/ACCA/CIPFA/Qualified AAT			Payroll clerk		
	Min	max	typical	Min	max	typical	Min	max	typical
Central London	80,000	110,000	85,000	20,500	30,000	26,000	15,000	21,000	17,500
Greater London	80,000	100,000	85,000	20,000	28,000	25,000	15,000	20,000	17,000
South Coast/Kent	70,000	85,000	80,000	18,000	28,000	25,500	14,500	19,500	17,500
Southern Home Counties	60,000	75,000	65,000	15,000	28,000	25,000	14,000	20,000	17,000
Northern Home Counties	62,000	80,000	70,000	17,500	28,000	24,000	15,000	20,000	17,000
Thames Valley	60,000	110,000	75,000	17,000	29,000	24,000	11,500	17,000	16,000
East Anglia	50,000	68,000	60,000	17,000	25,000	23,000	13,500	19,000	16,500
Midlands	45,000	85,000	61,000	15,000	24,000	21,000	10,000	16,000	14,200
South West	46,000	72,000	59,000	16,000	22,000	20,000	11,000	15,000	12,500
Wales	40,000	49,500	44,000	14,000	20,000	18,000	13,000	16,500	16,000
North West	46,000	61,000	54,000	16,000	21,000	19,000	13,000	15,000	14,000
North East/Yorks	45,000	65,000	55,000	15,000	19,200	18,000	14,000	17,600	16,000
Scotland	40,000	65,000	52,000	15,000	19,000	17,000	11,500	15,000	14,000
Nat average			65,000			21,625			15,642

MEDIUM HOUSING ASSOCIATIONS

	Finance director			Part-qualified accountant			Payroll clerk		
	Min	max	typical	Min	max	typical	Min	max	typical
Central London	50,000	70,000	65,000	24,000	29,000	26,500	15,500	20,000	16,500
Greater London	50,000	70,000	65,000	22,000	28,000	25,000	15,000	20,000	16,000
South Coast/Kent	50,000	65,000	55,000	23,000	28,000	24,500	14,000	20,000	16,000
Southern Home Counties	43,000	54,000	43,000	20,000	28,000	24,000	13,000	20,000	17,000
Northern Home Counties	38,000	50,000	43,000	25,000	28,000	26,000	15,000	19,000	17,500
Thames Valley	44,000	70,000	50,000	25,000	28,000	25,500	16,000	22,000	17,750
East Anglia	40,000	55,000	45,000	18,000	24,000	20,000	11,000	16,000	14,500
Midlands	33,000	62,000	50,000	12,000	21,000	19,500	9,500	18,000	14,500
South West	38,000	51,000	44,000	14,000	24,000	18,000	11,000	13,000	12,000
Wales	35,000	47,000	40,000	14,200	21,000	18,000	10,500	13,500	12,000
North West	29,000	40,000	33,000	15,000	18,000	17,000	13,000	17,000	15,500
North East/Yorks	33,000	37,000	35,000	15,000	17,500	17,000	12,500	17,000	15,500
Scotland	31,000	40,000	34,500	16,500	24,500	19,000	11,000	14,500	12,000
Nat average			46,346			21,125			15,021

SMALL HOUSING ASSOCIATIONS

	Finance director			Assistant accountant			Payroll clerk		
	Min	max	typical	Min	max	typical	Min	max	typical
Central London	40,000	55,000	50,000	19,000	28,000	23,000	15,500	20,000	16,500
Greater London	40,000	50,000	45,000	19,000	25,000	22,000	14,000	18,000	16,000
South Coast/Kent	30,000	50,000	42,000	15,000	25,000	21,500	13,500	18,000	15,500
Southern Home Counties	35,000	45,000	40,000	20,000	26,000	23,000	13,000	18,000	16,000
Northern Home Counties	35,000	45,000	40,000	19,000	25,000	22,000	13,500	18,000	16,000
Thames Valley	35,000	55,000	41,000	18,000	24,500	23,000	12,750	17,500	15,750
East Anglia	32,000	47,000	39,000	18,500	24,750	22,000	12,750	17,000	15,000
Midlands	30,000	52,000	45,000	13,500	22,000	19,000	10,000	16,000	14,200
South West	34,000	42,000	37,500	17,000	21,000	18,000	12,000	18,000	14,000
Wales	28,000	42,000	36,000	16,000	19,000	17,500	12,000	15,500	14,000
North West	27,000	33,000	36,000	16,000	21,000	18,000	11,000	17,000	14,500
North East/Yorks	27,500	42,000	37,000	15,700	17,500	16,000	12,700	14,700	14,500
Scotland	26,000	40,000	34,000	15,000	18,000	17,000	11,000	15,000	12,500
Nat average			40,192			19,917			14,829

Data supplied by HaysWorks.com

PAY

Housing associations do not have jointly agreed pay rates for particular jobs. Each association will fix its own. However, they will be careful to look at what the market seems to be for particular positions every year, and keep an eye on what other similar employers pay. It's worth remembering that pay itself is only one part of what motivates people to go to work, and this is especially true for people in the housing world.

It's relatively secure work, as well as offering variety. Employers are likely to follow the best practice available when setting their policies for staff recruitment and retention.

As a big generalisation, in the urban areas, housing organisations are likely to pay towards the upper end of the range for jobs that are similar to those in the private sector – for example customer services and finance assistant jobs. Young graduates with a housing qualification and some experience working in central London might expect to earn around £20,000.

At more senior levels the position changes. The director of a housing department or chief executive of a housing association would probably earn less than someone with equivalent strategic, budgeting and staff responsibilities in the private sector. Obviously working in the public or voluntary sector means that people do not have the 'profit motive' driving what they do. The annual budget has to fit all sorts of externally driven standards, and the main source of income, rents, is controlled by government guidelines. Where salaries are essentially funded from rents and public grants pay levels will not be exceptional, but they will be fair to the market. But there are many other great satisfiers in this kind of work.

OTHER BENEFITS

However, when looking for a career it is very important to think about aspects of the 'benefit package', as it is sometimes called, not just the amount of pay in the bank at the end of the month in your first job.

'COFEM'

Career opportunities for people from ethnic minorities
In the North West a group of housing associations got together to look at ways of helping black and minority ethnic staff develop their careers in housing. This is part of their commitment to making sure that every one has equal opportunity to personal and career development. They arrange secondments (where staff from one organisation go and work for a time in another organisation to widen their experience), mentoring (where young people get the chance to be guided and coached by experienced senior staff) and have a website with job, training and 'networking opportunities' – which means getting to know lots of other people working in housing and related jobs.

More information can be found at: www.cofem.org.uk

Housing organisations are likely to be decent employers, with effective equal opportunities policies. They will probably offer pension contributions. They may pay for private health insurance – or at least for eye tests and screening. Paid annual holiday may be more generous than in the private sector, and while paid overtime is not common staff may be able to take time off in lieu of evening or weekend work.

Housing organisations are quite likely to be responsive to the needs of staff who take maternity leave or who have responsibility for caring for children or dependent relatives. They may be willing to offer flexible working arrangements such as job-sharing or part time or flexi-time. Some are now using the opportunities offered by IT so their staff can work from home.

TRAINING AND PERSONAL DEVELOPMENT

Many housing organisations now have Investors in People accreditation, which means they take special care to train and develop their staff for the good of their business. It is now usual for all staff to have at least an annual appraisal that will help identify their training and personal development needs and preferences for the future. Many organisations will offer regular in-house training and attendance at short courses and conferences. Some will let you 'job swap' to find out more about the different kinds of work available.

Larger organisations may offer in-house career development. You might for example start off as a receptionist, then move on to become a housing assistant, and be encouraged to study for a professional qualification with a view to promotion to housing officer when a vacancy comes up.

CASE STUDY

Dyane Kesto, London and Quadrant Housing Association Millennium trainee

Dyane tells her story

Well my family and I left Wolverhampton, West Midlands for a fresh start in life. We heard that London had lots of job opportunities, while living in a small town like Wolverhampton jobs were scarce. We moved to London in July 1999.

The first week of us moving I went to the Jobcentre and careers office to look for work. I finally found work with an agency. Two months after I started work I had a letter from L&Q saying I had an interview. I was surprised because I didn't remember filling in a form for L&Q.

I went for the interview and realised when I got there that at the careers centre I had been told to fill in a form. 'This is a good one' the lady in the centre had told me. She told me nothing about it so I just filled in the form.

The interview went OK because I got the post, and I was told it was for a Millennium Trainee. They told me what it involved, which was to complete an NVQ course, which I wasn't looking forward to.

But I soon realised that doing a course didn't have to be boring. I really enjoyed doing it, and I completed it too. I also got to work in other departments, for example the department I found the most exciting was Customer Services, where I was the first port of call for the tenants and each tenant had a different case. Some of them were nice and polite, others were not, which also helped me with personal skills I was lacking in.

This was a big part in my decision to stay with the trust. I enjoyed what I had learnt, wanted to better my skills, and I thought L&Q was the best place to better myself. Since working for the trust I have gained a great deal of confidence.

The most important thing that the training I had taught me is: 'We all know that we should put the customer first and a good training programme tells you what that means; it shows you how.'

An enormous range of support for staff who want to take professional qualifications while at work may be offered. Housing organisations may give paid day release or block release for approved courses, which might range in discipline from housing management to accountancy. Leave for study and exams may be granted, as may financial help for study materials such as books and journals.

Annual subscriptions may be paid for staff who are qualified in a relevant profession. Although you might have to agree to stay on for a year or two if your employer has supported you in getting a qualification it is not at all uncommon to train yourself up with one employer and then move on to a more senior job elsewhere.

Summing up, then, public and voluntary bodies aim to offer pay and benefits to staff appropriate to the 'non-profit' sector. There will be no share options or big bonuses! But there are usually significant other benefits on offer – in addition to the prospect of job satisfaction and an enjoyable working environment. It's not a big world, and you tend to make good friends who you'll come across again and again as you move from job to job within the sector.

Above all, if you are at the start of your working life you should think about the enormous flexibility that starting off in housing will offer you. The next chapter talks about some of the relevant qualifications and other disciplines. If you find after a while that housing management itself is not up your street you will be well positioned to change direction with good experience under your belt.

Chapter 12
PROFESSIONAL AND OTHER QUALIFICATIONS

Throughout this book we have seen that all sorts of different kinds of jobs contribute to organisations that provide and manage housing. Starting as a school leaver, or as someone returning to work after a career break, is no barrier at all to promotion, career development and eventually taking a relevant professional qualification when you know what sort of work appeals to you and suits you best.

There are a large number of university courses in housing or in closely related disciplines. A fantastically high proportion – more than 90 per cent – of graduates get jobs in housing within 6 months of leaving a full-time degree or postgraduate course.

For the core discipline of managing property, qualifications approved by the Chartered Institute of Housing are likely to be the most relevant.

What is the Chartered Institute of Housing?
This is the professional association for all those working, studying or with an interest in housing. Currently there are more than 17,000 members. It is a registered charity that exists continually to improve standards within the housing profession. As well as its role in education, the CIH runs conferences, training and events, produces publications and guidance. Its Good Practice Unit helps disseminate ideas and information and its policy work helps shape government thinking. The CIH has offices in England, Scotland, Wales, Northern Ireland and Hong Kong. There are active regional branches that run their own events and training. CIH members include housing officers, tenants, caretakers, repairs staff, housing academics, private sector landlords, board members and councillors with a wide range of positions and experience – all sharing a common interest in housing.

LEVEL 2 CERTIFICATE IN HOUSING

A Level 2 Certificate in Housing course has been designed for people who have left school and who either want to work towards the National Certificate in Housing or the Professional Qualification, or who just want to have a better understanding of what housing is all about. It is a level 2 vocationally related qualification. There are four units to the course:

1. What is Housing
2. Communication skills for housing
3. Personal development for people in housing
4. Participating in housing.

To give you an idea of what this involves, the guidance from the CIH is that you have to complete all four units to get the certificate, and each unit needs probably 30 hours learning.

Once the certificate has been achieved you can choose to study other level 2 qualifications or you can go on to various NVQ level 3 opportunities. These include:

- CIH National Certificate in Housing
- Other level 3 opportunities within housing associated areas such as care
- Other level 3 opportunities outside housing.

The level 2 Certificate in Housing can also help if you want to gain key skills qualifications. There are three main key skills that are useful to have whatever career you want to pursue:

- Communication
- Application of number
- Information technology.

There are also three 'wider' key skills:

- Working with others
- Improving own learning and performance
- Problem solving.

All of these key skills can be studied at four levels of increasing demand.

Housing Potential UK

The learning and skills council for housing (Housing Potential UK) is responsible for providing strategic guidance on how to deliver education and training to people working in the rented housing sector. This is also the awarding body for the key skills qualification. Housing Potential has prepared a plan for government to show what needs to be done to equip the workforce in housing with the expertise and training it needs to meet the constant changes and challenges of the work ahead. You can find out more about it through its website www.housingpotential.com, where you will find:

- the new housing occupational standards;
- Britain's largest database of searchable housing training containing over 1000 courses from over 100 providers;
- 'Training Together' – research into training across the housing care divide;
- the housing sector workforce development plan – the basis for action and funding fo staff development in housing organisations;
- a range of news, research, features and reports covering good practice in the recruitment, retention and development of staff.

Try the Qualifications and Curriculum Authority too, at www.qca.org.uk

THE NATIONAL CERTIFICATE IN HOUSING

Once eligible, you might want to do further study in a particular housing topic. Topics include:

- Supported housing
- Tenant participation
- Housing management and maintenance
- Housing aid and advice
- Benefits.

You study six core units common to all areas of housing and six pathway units on specialised subjects.

Beyond that there are higher certificates in specialised work such as student accommodation management. The certificates usually require you to complete four study modules , together with demonstrating what you have learned in your practical experience of the subject at work. The work is level 3 – A level standard.

COURSES LEADING TO THE CIH PROFESSIONAL QUALIFICATION

If you decide you want to go on and study for the full professional qualification there are a number of routes you might take. One is through taking the Higher National Certificate in Housing Studies. This forms the first part of the CIH Professional Qualification and, like many other courses, can be studied by distance learning.

Study by distance learning suits well people who are already working or live a long way from the colleges offering housing courses. You are allocated a personal tutor and will also have to attend a limited number of day courses, but mostly you will be working from home. Check whether you live or work close to one of the educational establishments that offer relevant courses – there are 91 in the UK. To find out more you will need to contact the CIH Education Department on 024 7685 1776.

The academic part of the professional qualification is studied at undergraduate or postgraduate level. If you already have NVQ/SVQ level 4 you will be recognised as meeting the requirements of Stage 1 of the professional qualification. You can also reach it by completing the first part of an undergraduate award leading to a diploma or BSc/BA in Housing or the HNC in Housing.

The second stage of the CIH Professional Qualification is the professional diploma or BA/BSc in housing. These courses are offered by a number of universities and colleges across the UK, and can also be taken by distance learning through the union UNISON and through the CIH's own distance learning centre (dlc@cih.org).

Undergraduate and postgraduate courses in housing and related studies

Housing as a profession has no entry requirements as such, and you may get a job from which you can study part-time, perhaps with support from your employer for day-release, if you want to qualify. If you want to on to study after leaving school but want to work as well, or are thinking about working part-time while studying, there are related courses at universities and colleges all over the country, from Amersham to Ystrad Mynach! And 90 per cent of graduates get relevant jobs in the first six months. The Chartered Institute of Housing publishes a list of courses available, but it is a good idea to check with colleges direct for details.

If you have a first degree, and want to go on to do professional qualifications but work as well, there are ways to do both. At the University of Salford, for example, you can do an MSc, studying during year one from September till May, then doing a work placement in year two. This helps the employer by ensuring staff get full professional development and of course it is good for the staff who will get better career opportunities through the qualifications they receive. And 30 per cent of those MSc students are in promoted posts within two years.

Some postgraduate courses are also recognised by the Institute as meeting Stage 1 and Stage 2 of the professional qualification. You might have to take a graduate conversion course if your first degree is not in a subject thought to be relevant.

Levels of the National Qualifications Framework	Housing Qualifications	Other Qualifications
Level 5	CIH Professional Qualification	Masters degrees Honours degrees
Level 4	CIH Higher National Certificate in Housing CIH Higher Certificates NVQ/SVQ in Housing BTEC Higher National Certificate in Housing	Early stages of undergraduate programmes
Level 3	CIH National Certificate in Housing NVQ/SVQ in Housing	GCE A Level Scottish Highers/Higher Still
Level 2	CIH Level 2 Certificate NVQ/SVQ in Housing	GCSE Scottish Standard Grades

Finally, to become eligible to be a full corporate member of the CIH, candidates have to complete a Test of Professional Practice, called APEX, which demonstrates the candidate's practical understanding of housing service delivery.

While most professional members of the Institute become qualified by the processes described above there is a fast track for people who are professionally qualified in other disciplines. So if you are reading this book because you are thinking about a career change, or you want to come into housing after a career break, you might already be qualified in one of these areas:

- Chartered Association of Certified Accountants
- Chartered Institute of Bankers (incorporating the Chartered Building Societies Institute)
- Chartered Institute of Building
- Chartered Institute of Environmental Health Officers
- Chartered Institute of Management Accountants
- Chartered Institute of Personal Development
- Chartered Institute of Public Finance and Accountancy
- Incorporated Society of Valuers and Auctioneers
- Institute of Chartered Accountants
- Institute of Chartered Secretaries and Administrators
- Institute of Civil Engineers
- Institute of Cost Management and Management Accountants
- Institute of Legal Executives
- The Law Society
- Royal Environmental Health Institute of Scotland
- Royal Institute of British Architects
- Royal Institute of Chartered Surveyors
- Royal Town Planning Institute

or

- MBA/Diploma in Management Studies
- NVQ/SVQ level 5
- Three-year officer training course provided by the RAF
- Diploma in Social Work approved by the Central Council for Education and Training in Social Work (CCETSW)

- University of Leicester MA in the Management of Partnerships and Collaboration.

The CIH is also committed to the ongoing professional development of all those working in housing, so even once you are qualified, you are likely to go on expanding your knowledge and keeping up to date with the many legal and other changes which will happen during your working life in housing.

For more information contact:

The Chartered Institute of Housing (CIH)
Octavia House
Westwood Way
Coventry CV4 8JP
Tel: 024 7685 1700
Fax: 024 7669 5110
Email: customer.services@cih.org
Web: www.cih.org

Chapter 13
DIRECTORY

WHERE TO FIND OUT MORE

If you think you might be interested in finding out more about housing there are a number of journals and magazines that carry information, articles and, crucially, job advertisements. Look at these carefully; they will give you up-to-date guidance about job prospects. Most housing organisations advertise widely and have a thorough process for assessing applications and carrying out interviews. They are careful about providing equality of opportunity and will make a fair assessment of the merits of all applications. Sending your CV in 'on spec' will probably not get you very far. Some specialised jobs may be recruited to through agencies. These are included in the addresses in the following section.

But, to start, try:

Careers Services Local services, both municipal and private or voluntary, will be listed in the local press or at public libraries, in schools or colleges. As well as advice, some services offer guidance on CV compilation, letter writing and jobsearch techniques.

Chartered Institute of Housing www.cih.org.

Council for Voluntary Services Local branch addresses can be found in the local press or in public libraries. Coordinates voluntary activities in the area. Voluntary work in the housing field is regarded as evidence of commitment as well as useful experience.

Guardian The *Guardian* newspaper on Wednesdays specialises in advertising jobs in housing, social care and related areas in a supplement, 'Society'.

Inside Housing www.insidehousing.co.uk Weekly magazine for housing professionals – contains jobs section as well as useful news on current housing issues.

Opportunities, Opportunities, Link House, West Street, Poole, Dorset BH15 1LL, www.opportunities.co.uk Weekly newsletter specialising in employment opportunities in local government.

USEFUL ADDRESSES

Age Concern (England)
Astral House
1268 London Road
London SW16 4ER
Tel: 020 8679 8000
Fax: 020 8679 6069
Email: ace@ace.org.uk
Web: www.ace.org.uk

Age Concern (Cymru)
4th Floor
1 Cathedral Road
Cardiff CF11 9SD
Tel: 029 2037 1566
Fax: 029 2039 9562
Email: enquiries@accymru.org.uk
Web: www.accymru.org.uk

Age Concern (Northern Ireland)
3 Lower Crescent
Belfast BT7 1NR
Tel: 028 9024 5729
Email: ageconcern.ni@btinternet.com

Age Concern (Scotland)
113 Rose Street
Edinburgh EH2 3DT
Tel: 0131 220 3345
Fax: 0131 220 2779
Email: enquiries@acsinfo3.freeserve.co.uk

Alzheimer's Society
Gordon House

10 Greencoat Place
London SW1P 1PH
Tel: 020 7306 0606
Fax: 020 7306 0808
Email: info@alzheimers.org.uk
Web: www.alzheimers.org.uk

ARLA (Association of Residential Letting Agents)
Maple House
53–55 Woodside Road
Amersham
Bucks HP6 6AA
Tel: 0845 345 5752
Fax: 01494 431530
Email: info@arla.co.uk

Association of Residential Management Agents
178 Battersea Park Road
London SW11 4ND
Tel: 020 7978 2607
Fax: 020 7498 6153
Email: info@arma.org.uk
Web: www.arma.org.uk

The Association of Retirement Housing Managers
3rd floor
Albert Embankment
London SE1 7TP
Tel and Fax: 020 7820 1839
Email: enquiries@arhm.org
Web: www.arhm.org

Audit Commission
1 Vincent Square
London SW1P 2PN
Tel: 020 7828 1212
Fax: 020 7976 6187
Email: enquiries@audit-commission.gov.uk
Web: www.audit-commission.gov.uk/

Getting into Housing

Audit Commission in Wales
4th Floor
Deri House
2–4 Park Grove
Cardiff CF10 3ZZ
Tel: 029 2026 2550
Fax: 029 2039 7070
Web: www.audit-commission.gov.uk/

Audit Scotland
110 George Street
Edinburgh EH2 4LH
Tel: 0131 477 1234
Fax: 0131 477 4567
Email: info@audit-scot.gov.uk
Web: www.audit-scotland.gov.uk.

Building Societies Association
3 Savile Row
London W1S 3PB
Tel: 020 7437 0655
Fax: 020 7734 6416
Email: name@bsa.org.uk
Web: www.bsa.org.uk/

Care and Repair England
3rd Floor, Bridgford House
Pavilion Road
West Bridgford
Nottingham NG2 5GJ
Tel: 0115 982 1527
Fax: 0115 982 1529
Email: info@careandrepair-england.org.uk
Web: www.careandrepair-england.org.uk/

Care and Repair Cymru
Norbury House
Norbury Road

Fairwater
Cardiff CF5 3AS
Tel: 029 2057 6286
Fax: 029 2057 6283
Web: www.careandrepair.org.uk

Catholic Housing Aid Society
209 Old Marylebone Road
London NW1 5QT
Tel: 020 7723 7273
Fax: 020 7723 5943
Email: info@chasnational.org.uk
Web: www.chasnational.org.uk

CECODHAS (European Liaison Committee for Social Housing)
Executive Secretary
Tineke Zuidervaart
Aedes, Hilversum,
The Netherlands
Olympia 1
NL - 1213 NS HILVERSUM
Tel: (+) 31 35 626 83 33
Fax: (+) 31 35 626 84 33
Email: ir@aedesnet.nl
Web: www.cecodhas.org
Representative in Brussels
Claire Roumet
40 Rue des Colonies
B - 1000 BRUXELLES
Tel: (+) 32 2 505 45 00
Fax: (+) 32 2 505 44 99
Email: cecodhas@vhm.be

Centre for Housing Management and Development
College of Cardiff
University of Wales
Dept of City and Regional Planning
PO Box 906

Cardiff CF1 3YN
Tel: 029 2087 4000
Fax: 029 2087 4845
Web: www.cardiff.ac.uk

Centre for Housing Policy
University of York
Heslington
York
YO10 5DD
Tel: 01904 433691
Fax: 01904 432318
Email: mj12@york.ac.uk
Web: www.york.ac.uk/inst/chp/

Centre for Urban and Regional Studies
J G Smith Building
The University of Birmingham
Edgbaston
Birmingham B15 2TT
General Enquiries:
Tel: 0121 414 5021
Fax: 0121 414 3279
Email: name@bham.ac.uk
Web: www.spp3.bham.ac.uk/curs/

Centre for Regional Economic and Social Research
School of Environment and Development
Sheffield Hallam University
City Campus
Sheffield S1 1WB
Tel: 0114 225 4267
Fax: 0114 225 3179
Email sed@shu.ac.uk
Web: www.shu.ac.uk/cresr/ for Regional Economic and Social Research

Centrepoint
Neil House
7 Whitechapel Road

London E1 1DU
Tel: 020 7426 5300
Fax: 020 7426 5301
Email: name@centrepoint.org.uk
Web: www.centrepoint.org.uk

Chartered Institute of Building
Englemere
Kings Ride
Ascot
Berks SL5 7TB
Tel: 01344 630700
Fax: 01344 630777
Email: rcccption@ciob.org.uk
Web: www.ciob.org.uk

Chartered Institute of Environmental Health
Chadwick Court
15 Hatfields
London SE1 8DJ
Tel: 020 7928 6006
Fax: 020 7827 5866
Email: cieh@cieh.org
Web: www.cieh.org.uk/

Chartered Institute of Housing (CIH)
Headquarters
Octavia House
Westwood Way
Coventry CV4 8JP
Tel: 024 7685 1700
Fax: 024 7669 5110
Email: customer.services@cih.org
Web: www.cih.org

CIH in Scotland
Tel: 0131 225 4544
Fax: 0131 225 4566
Email: scotland@cih.org and scotland.training@cih.org

CIH Cymru
Tel: 029 2076 5760
Fax: 029 2076 5761
Email: cymru@cih.org and cymru.training@cih.org

CIH in Northern Ireland
Tel: 028 9077 8222
Fax: 028 9077 8333
Email: ni@cih.org and ni.training@cih.org

CIH London Office
Tel: 020 7837 4280
Fax: 020 7278 2705
Email: london@cih.org and press@cih.org

CIH Asia Pacific
Tel: (00) 852 2356 8680
Fax: (00) 852 2356 733
Email: nbk@cih.org.hk

CIH – Careers
Tel: 024 7685 1788
Email: careers@cih.org

CIH – Education
Tel: 024 7685 1776
Fax: 024 7646 4928
Email: education@cih.org

CIH – Distance Learning Centre
Tel; 024 7685 1700
Fax: 024 7669 4209
Email: dlc@cih.org

CIH – Training England
Tel: 024 7685 1772
Fax: 024 7642 1973
Email: england.training@cih.org

Chartered Institute of Public Finance and Accountancy
3 Robert Street
London WC2N 6RL.
Tel: 020 7543 5600
Fax: 020 7543 5700
Email:first.lastname@cipfa.org.uk
Web: www.cipfa.org.uk/

Child Poverty Action Group
94 White Lion Street
London N1 9PF
Tel: 020 7837 7979
Fax: 020 7837 6414
Email: staff@cpag.demon.co.uk
Web: www.cpag.org.uk/

Communities Scotland
91 Haymarket Terrace
Edinburgh EH12 5HE
Tel: 0131 313 0044
Fax: 0131 313 2680
Web: www.commitiesscotland.gov.uk

Commission for Racial Equality
Elliot House
10–12 Allington Street
London SW1E 5EH
Tel: 0207 828 7022
Fax: 0207 630 7605
Email: info@cre.gov.uk
Web: www.cre.gov.uk/

Crisis
Warwick House
25–27 Buckingham Palace Road
London SW1W OPP
1st Floor
Tel: 08700 113335

Email: firstname.lastname@crisis.org.uk
Web: www.crisis.org.uk

Department for Transport, Local Government and the Regions (DTLR)
Eland House
Bressenden Place
London SW1E 5DU
Tel: 020 7944 3000
Email: housing@dtlr.gov.uk
Web: www.dtlr.gov.uk

DTLR Regional Offices:

Department for Social Development for Northern Ireland
Churchill House
Victoria Square
Belfast BT1 4SD
Tel: 028 9056 9100
Web: www.dsdni.gov.uk

Empty Homes Agency
195–197 Victoria Street
London SW1E 5NE
Tel: 020 7828 6288
Fax: 020 7828 7006
Email: info@emptyhomes.com
Web: www.emptyhomes.com

Equal Opportunities Commission
Arndale House
Arndale Centre
Manchester M4 3EQ
Tel: 08456 015901
Fax: 0161 838 8312
Email: info@eoc.org.uk
Web: www.eoc.org.uk/

Federation of Black Housing Organisations Ltd
2nd floor
1 King Edwards Road

London E9 7SF
Tel: 020 8533 7053
Fax: 020 8985 9166
Email: fbho@teleregion.co.uk

The Foyer Federation
Second Floor
Humatt House
146–148 Clerkenwell Road
London EC1R 5DG
Tel: 020 7833 8616
Fax: 020 7833 8717
Email: federation@foyer.net
Web: www.foyer.net

Help the Aged
207–221 Pentonville Road
London N1 9UZ
Tel: 020 7278 1114
Fax: 020 7278 1116
Email: info@helptheaged.org.uk
Web: www.helptheaged.org.uk/

Homeless International
Queens House
16 Queens Road
Coventry CV1 3DF
Tel: 024 7663 2802
Fax: 024 7663 2911
Email: info@homeless-international.org
Web: www.homeless-international.org/

Homeless Link
Alliance House
12 Caxton Street
London SW1H 0QS
Tel: 020 7799 2404
Fax: 020 7976 7248
Email: hn@homelesslink.org.uk
Web: www.homelesslink.org.co.uk

HOMES (Housing Organisations Mobility and Exchange Services)
242 Vauxhall Bridge Road
London SW1V 1AU
Tel: 020 7963 0200
Fax: 020 7963 0249
Email: customer.services@homes.org.uk
Web: www.homes.org.uk/

HouseMark Online Services Ltd
Unit 8 Mercia Business Village
Torwood Close
Westwood Business Park
Coventry CV4 8HX
Tel: 024 7646 0500
Fax: 024 7646 0093
Email: info@housemark.co.uk
Web: www.housemark.co.uk

Housing Corporation (England)
Corporate Services
Maple House
149 Tottenham Court Road
London W1P 0BN
Tel: 020 7393 2000
Fax: 020 7393 2111
Email: enquiries@housingcorp.gsx.gov.uk
Web: www.housingcorp.gov.uk/

Housing Law Practitioners Association
120 Wilton Road
London SW1V 1JZ
Tel: 020 7233 8322
Fax: 020 7233 7779
Email: profbriefings@msn.com
Web: www.profbriefings.co.uk/assoc/hlpa.htm

Housing Potential UK Ltd
PO Box 1581
Octavia House

Westwood Way
Coventry CV4 8ZE
Tel: 024 7685 1796
Fax: 024 7669 5389
Email: info@housingpotential.com

Independent Housing Ombudsman Ltd
Norman House
105-109 Strand
London WC2R 0AA
Tel: 020 7836 3630
Fax: 020 7836 3900
Email: ombudsman@ihos.org.uk
Web: www.ihos.org.uk/

Institute of Maintenance and Building Management
Keets House
30 East Street
Farnham
Surrey GU9 7SW
Tel: 01252 710994
Fax: 01252 737741
Email: imbm@btconnect.com
Web: www.imbm.org.uk/

Institute of Residential Property Management
178 Battersea Park Road
London SW11 4ND
Tel: 020 7622 5092
Fax: 020 7498 6153
Email: info@irpm.org.uk
Web: www.irpm.org.uk

Joseph Rowntree Foundation
The Homestead
40 Water End
York, North Yorkshire
YO30 6WP
Tel: 01904 629241

Getting into Housing

Fax: 01904 620072
Email: info@jrf.org.uk
Web: www.jrf.org.uk/

Learning and Skills Council HQ
101 Lockhurst Lane
Foles Hill
Coventry CV6 5SF
Tel: 0845 019 4170
Web: www.lsc.gov.uk

Leasehold Advisory Service
70–74 City Road
London EC1Y 2BJ
Tel: 020 7490 9580
Fax: 020 7253 2043
Email: info@lease-advice.org
Web: www.lease-advice.org.uk

Local Government Association
Local Government House
Smith Square
London SW1P 3HZ
Tel: 020 7664 3000
Fax: 020 7664 3030
Email: info@lga.gov.uk
Web: www.lga.gov.uk/

London Housing Unit
Association of London Government
59 and a half Southwark Street
London SE1 0AL
Tel: 020 7934 9811
Email: info-lhu@alg.gov.uk
Web: www.lhu.org.uk/

London Voluntary Service Council
356 Holloway Road
London N7 6PA

Tel: 020 7700 8107
Fax: 020 7700 8108
Minicom: 020 7700 8163
Information service and library tel: 020 7700 8104
Email: lvsc@lvsc.org.uk
Web: www.lvsc.org.uk

Mencap
123 Golden Lane
London EC1Y 0RT
Tel: 020 7454 0454
Fax: 020 7696 5540
Email: information@mencap.org.uk
Web: www.mencap.org.uk

Mencap Cymru
31 Lambourne Crescent
Cardiff Business Park
Llanishen
Cardiff CF14 5GF
Tel: 029 2074 7588
Fax: 029 2074 7550
Email: information.wales@mencap.org.uk

Mencap in Northern Ireland
Segal House
4 Annadale Avenue
Belfast BT7 3JH
Tel: 028 9069 1351
Fax: 028 9064 0121
Email: mencapni@mencap.org.uk

Mind
15–19 Broadway
London E15 4BQ
Tel: 020 8519 2122
Fax: 020 8522 1725
Email: contact@mind.org.uk
Web: www.mind.org.uk

Getting into Housing

National Assembly for Wales
Housing
Cathays Park
Cardiff CF10 3NQ
Tel: 029 2082 5111
Fax: 029 2092 5136
Web: www.wales.gov.uk

NACRO (National Association for the Care and Resettlement of
Offenders)
169 Clapham Road
London SW9 0PU
Tel: 020 7582 6500
Fax: 020 7735 4666
Email: firstname.lastname@nacro.org.uk
Web: www.nacro.org.uk/

National Association of Citizens Advice Bureaux
115/123 Pentonville Road
London N1 9LZ
Tel: 020 7833 2181
Fax: 020 7833 4371
Email: firstname.lastname@nacab.org.uk
Web: www.nacab.org.uk/

National Council for Voluntary Organisations (NCVO)
Regent's Wharf
8 All Saints Street
London N1 9RL
Tel: 020 7713 6161
Fax: 020 7713 6300
Minicom: 0800 01 88 111
Helpdesk: 0800 2 798 798
Email: ncvo@ncvo-vol.org.uk
Web: www.ncvo-vol.org.uk

National Housing Federation
175 Gray's Inn Road

London
WC1X 8UP
Tel: 020 7278 6571
Fax: 020 7833 8323
Email: info@housing.org.uk
Web: www.housing.org.uk/

National Wardens Association
Katepwa House
Ashfield Park Avenue
Ross-on-Wye
Herefordshire
HR9 5AX
Tel: 01989 566699
Fax: 01989 567676
Email:nwa@assocmanagement.co.uk

Northern Ireland Federation of Housing Associations
38 Hill Street
Belfast
BT1 2LB
Tel: 028 9023 0446
Fax: 028 9023 8057
Email: info@nifha.org
Web: www.nifha.org/

Northern Ireland Housing Executive
The Housing Centre
2 Adelaide Street
Belfast BT2 8PB
Tel: 028 9024 0588
Fax: 028 9031 8008
Email: info@nihe.gov.uk
Web: www.nihe.gov.uk/

Northern Ireland Office
Block B, Castle Buildings
Belfast BT4 3SG

Tel: 028 9052 0700
Fax: 028 9052 8195
Email: press.nio@nics.gov.uk
Web: www.nio.gov.uk/

Northern Ireland Tenants Action Project (NITAP)
PO Box 131
Ballymena BT43 6BD
Tel: 028 2564 5676
Fax: 028 2564 9729
Email: info@nitap.org
Web: www.nitap.org

PATH National (Positive Action for Training in Housing)
Whittington House
764–768 Holloway Road
London N19 3JG
Tel: 020 7281 8001
Email:name@pathuk.co.uk

People for Action
138 Digbeth
Birmingham B5 6DR
Tel: 0121 633 3836
Fax: 0121 633 3882
Email: info@peopleforaction.demon.co.uk
Web: www.peopleforaction.org.uk

Property Managers Association Scotland Ltd
2 Blythswood Square
Glasgow
G2 4AD
Tel: 0141 248 4672
Fax: 0141 221 9270
Email: Jamie.millar@morisonbishop.co.uk

Qualification and Curriculum Authority
83 Piccadilly
London W1J 8QA

Tel: 020 7509 5555
Fax: 020 7509 6944
Web: www.qca.org.uk/

The Rent Service
Headquarters and policy
First Floor
Clifton House
87-113 Euston Road
LONDON NW1 2RA
Tel: 020 7554 2450
Web site: www.therentservice.gov.uk

ROOM (National Council for Housing and Planning)
14 Old Street
London EC1V 9BH
Tel: 020 7251 2363
Fax: 020 7608 2830
Email: mail@room.org.uk
Web: www.room.org.uk/

Royal Institution of Chartered Surveyors (RICS)
12 Great George Street
Parliament Square
London SW1P 3AD
Tel: 020 7222 7000
Fax: 020 7222 9430
Email: info@rics.org.uk
Web: www.rics.org.

Royal National Institute for the Blind (RNIB)
105 Judd Street
London
WC1H 9NE
Tel: 020 7388 1266
Fax: 020 7388 2034
Email: name@rnib.org.uk
Web: www.rnib.org.uk

Getting into Housing

RNIB Services Northern Ireland
Unit B, 40 Linenhall Street
Belfast BT2 8BG
Tel: 028 9032 9373
Fax: 028 9043 9118

RNIB Cymru
Trident Court
East Moors Road
Cardiff CF24 5TD
Tel: 029 2045 0440
Fax: 029 2044 9550

RNIB Scotland
Dunedin House
25 Ravelston Terrace
Edinburgh EH4 3TP
Tel 0131 311 8500
Fax 0131 311 8529

Royal National Institute for the Deaf (RNID)
19–23 Featherstone Street
London EC1Y 8SL
Tel: 020 7296 8000
Textphone: 020 7296 8001
Fax: 020 7296 8199
Email: informationline@rnid.org.uk
Web: www.rnid.org.uk

Rural Housing Trust
8 Graphite Square
Vauxhall Walk
London SE11 5EE
Tel: 020 7793 8114
Fax: 020 7793 8148
Email: info@ruralhousing.org.uk
Web: www.ruralhousing.org.uk

Scope
6 Market Road
London N7 9PW
Tel: 020 7619 7100
Email: name@scope.org.uk
Web: www.scope.org.uk

Scottish Council for Single Homeless
5th Floor
Wellgate House
200 Cowgate
Edinburgh EH1 1NQ
Tel: 0131 226 4382
Fax: 0131 225 4382
Email: enquiries@scsh.demon.co.uk
Web: www.scsh.co.uk/

Scottish Federation of Housing Associations
38 York Place
Edinburgh EH1 3HU
Tel: 0131 556 5777
Fax: 0131 557 6028
Email: sfha@sfha.co.uk
Web: www.sfha.co.uk/

Scottish Qualifications Authority
Hanover House
24 Douglas Street
Glasgow G2 7NQ
Tel: 0141 242 2214
Fax: 0141 242 2244
Email: helpdesk@sqa.org.uk
Web: www.sqa.org.uk/

Sense
11–13 Clifton Terrace
Finsbury Park
London N4 3SR

Tel: 020 7272 7774
Fax: 020 7272 6012
Minicom:020 7272 9648
Email: enquiries@sense.org.uk
Web: www.sense.org.uk

Sense Scotland
5th Floor
45 Finnieston Street
Glasgow G3 8JU
Tel: 0141 564 2444
Fax: 0141 564 2443
Minicom: 0141 2442
Email: info@sensescotland.org.uk
Web: www.sensescotland.org.uk

Sense Northern Ireland
Sense Family Centre
The Manor House
51 Mallusk Road
Mallusk
County Antrim BT36 4RU
Tel: 028 9083 3430
Fax: 028 9084 4232
Minicom: 028 9083 3430

Sense Cymru
5 Raleigh Walk
Brigantine Place
Atlantic Wharf
Cardiff CF10 4LN
Tel: 029 2045 7641
Fax: 029 2049 9644
Minicom: 029 2046 4125

Shelter
88 Old Street
London EC1V 9HU

Tel: 020 7505 4699
Email: info@shelter.org.uk
Web: www.shelter.org.uk/

Shelter (Scotland)
4th Floor
Scotiabank House
6 South Charlotte Street
Edinburgh EH2 4AW
Tel: 0131 473 7170
Fax: 0131 473 7199
Email: shelterscot@shelter.org.uk
Web: www.shelterscotland.org.uk/

Shelter (Cymru)
25 Walter Road
Swansea
West Glamorgan SA1 5NN
Tel: 01792 469400
Fax: 01792 460050
Web: www.sheltercymru.org.uk/

Small Landlords' Association
Tel: 020 7828 2445

Tenant Participation Advisory Service (TPAS) (England)
Brunswick House
Broad Street
Salford M6 5BZ
Tel: 0161 745 7903
Fax: 0161 745 9259
Email: info@tpas.org.uk
Web: www.tpas.org.uk/

TPAS (Scotland)
74/78 Saltermarket
Glasgow G1 5LD
Tel: 0141 552 3633
Fax: 0141 552 0073

TPAS (Cymru)
Second Floor
Transport House
1 Cathedral Road
Cardiff CF11 9SD
Tel: 029 2023 7303
Fax: 029 2034 5597
Email: enquiries@tpascymru.org.uk
Web: www.tpascymru.org.uk/

UNISON
1 Mabledon Place
London WC1H 9AJ
Tel: 020 7388 2366
Fax: 020 7387 6692
Email: initial.surname@unison.org.uk
Web: www.unison.org.uk/

Welsh Federation of Housing Associations
Norbury House
Norbury Road
Fairwater
Cardiff CF5 3AS
Tel: 029 2030 3150
Fax: 029 2056 0668
Email: wfha@welshhousing.org.uk
Web: www.welshhousing.org.uk/

Welsh Local Government Association
Local Government House
Drake Walk
Cardiff CF10 4LG
Tel: 029 20468600
Fax: 029 20468601
Email: info@wlga.gov.uk
Web: www.wlga.gov.uk/